ESSAYS ON HIS WORKS

WRITERS SERIES

ANTONIO D'ALFONSO AND JOSEPH PIVATO

Canada Council   Conseil des Arts
for the Arts   du Canada

ONTARIO ARTS COUNCIL
CONSEIL DES ARTS DE L'ONTARIO

Guernica Editions Inc. acknowledges the support of
The Canada Council for the Arts.
Guernica Editions Inc. acknowledges the support of
the Ontario Arts Council.

ALDEN NOWLAN

ESSAYS ON HIS WORKS

EDITED BY GREGORY M. COOK

GUERNICA

TORONTO • BUFFALO • CHICAGO • LANCASTER (U.K.)

2006

Gregory M. Cook, Guest editor
Guernica Editions Inc.
P.O. Box 117, Station P, Toronto (ON), Canada M5S 2S6
2250 Military Road, Tonawanda, N.Y. 14150-6000 U.S.A.

Distributors:
University of Toronto Press Distribution,
5201 Dufferin Street, Toronto (ON), Canada M3H 5T8

Gazelle, White Cross Mills, High Town, Lancaster LA1 1XS U.K.

Independent Publishers Group,
814 N. Franklin Street, Chicago, Il. 60610 U.S.A.

Typeset by Selina.
Printed in Canada.
First edition.

Legal Deposit — Fourth Quarter
National Library of Canada
Library of Congress Catalog Card Number: 2006929271
Library and Archives Canada Cataloguing in Publication
Alden Nowlan : essays on his works /
edited by Gregory M. Cook. — 1st ed.
(Writers series ; 19)
ISBN 1-55071-254-3
1. Nowlan, Alden, 1933-1983 — Criticism and interpretation.
I. Cook, Gregory M., 1942- II. Series: Writers series (Toronto, Ont.) ; 19
PS8527.O798Z52 2006   C811'.54   C2006-903609-8

CONTENTS

ACKNOWLEDGEMENTS

The editor wishes to thank those who made this book possible, principally the contributors: Geoffrey Cook, John Metcalf, Paul Milton, Thomas R. Smith, and David Adams Richards (each contribution is cited in the bibliography of this volume.) I am grateful also for the contributions made to Canadian literature by the journals *Canadian Literature,* the *Globe and Mail, Pottersfield Portfolio*, and *Studies in Canadian Literature* in which four of these essays first appeared, in addition to the Canadian and US publishers: The House of Anansi Press and The Thousands Press.

I appreciate the work of editor Joseph Pivato who, through his Canadian Studies web site at the University of Athabaska, recommended that I compile these essays. I am happy to count him and publisher Antonio D'Alfonso among the ranks of those who recognize the expanding reputation of Alden Nowlan's works. A special thanks is due photographer Kent Nason for one of his exquisite portraits of Alden Nowlan on the cover. Last, but not least, I thank my first reader in all things, Leslie Ann Jeffrey.

I dedicate this book to Fred Cogswell (1917-2004)
who encouraged me to meet Alden Nowlan in 1963

Introduction

"What it is like to be Alden Nowlan,"
in the Canadian class-scape

Gregory M. Cook

Oh, admit this, man, there's no point in poetry
if you with hold the truth
once you've come by it.
   "And He Wept Aloud, So That the Egyptians Heard It"
   Alden Nowlan, *Selected Poems* (40)

In 1963, with these three lines from the book that
will win the primary school dropout a Governor
General's Award for poetry five years later, I introduced Alden Nowlan in his first magazine interview
published in Canada. Truth telling was the primary
aesthetic for the most courageous confessional voice
in North American poetry in English. The beauty of
Nowlan's affirming principle is that it transcends
official history, accepted taste, and the lies of the
poet's time. It enunciates the primary need for
recognition as a human being, something Nowlan
learned from harsh experience. His early learning,
whether by reading or by hearing the oracular wisdom of his elders, was an experience of each
moment retold, as in "Afterword to Genesis," in *The
Mysterious Naked Man* (1969). Here he adopts the

point of view of the child about to be sacrificed by the father: "Yet the time came when the young man, Isaac, could not sleep / for remembering / how he had been made less than a woman, less than a child, / less than a slave," and waited to be "blotted out, swallowed up, made nothing" (80).

Having overcome that terror of his childhood, Nowlan was striding in mid-career on one of the occasions when he lamented his publishing output as compared to his boyhood role models – like Jack London at age eleven, Guy de Maupassant at age thirteen, or D. H. Lawrence at age sixteen. He wrote to me with the understated pride of a working-class poet, "I tell myself, many people with my background have become public charges." Of course, he finds his balance in the humour of his own blues: "What the hell, I can't be Shakespeare. I may as well do the best I can with Alden Nowlan, seeing the poor bastard is all I've got to work with (214)."

This is the secret of a great artist humbled by the process of throwing something holy before beasts as echoed in D. H. Lawrence's creed: "Writing for my sake." Nowlan repeatedly described the feeling of the artist exposing himself as the price, or measure, of art – with the conviction that revealing the truth is a heroic, if not a sacred, act. In a regular weekly newspaper column, which he filed with the *Telegraph-Journal* for fifteen years, Nowlan writes: "Ever since I got sick [with cancer of the thyroid in 1966] I've become less and less hypocritical and more and more honest. Since we're all of us going to be out of the world soon it seems silly not to tell one another what we really think and feel" (7 May 1969).

This classical principle of self-examination, which at first glance appears to be the antithesis of invention, cultivates Nowlan's comprehending and lucid voice in all its grace. This chaste – and chastising – first commandment for truth arrives, for example, in his 1959 account of the adult poet's visit to his father's "rough deal table," where the house flies – symbolizing the 'god of the poor and outcast" – were so thick that the poet was enraged and began attacking them with the *Family Herald*, until he realized he was embarrassing his father (41). The only invention in the published version appears to be the reference to his father as "my grandfather." This is what Nowlan would call a "beneficent lie." The fabrication is simply to protect from ridicule his father who, unlike both Nowlan's grandfathers, is still alive when the poem is published. The earliest manuscript copy in the Harriet Irving Library at University of New Brunswick, reads "my father," and concludes: "I would have eaten flies by the handful rather than / embarrass him" (Nowlan Collection).

Nowlan's portrayal of the working class father-figure as hero, and alternately as anti-hero, was one of the early themes that first attracted me to his works. The companion poem, "At the Mill," published with my interview in *Amethyst*, is no longer extant. It represents the earlier Nowlan in its fictional imitation of more conventional versifying. In its romantic voice "My father" sacrifices himself (including giving "three golden fingers") to his "god" (his Moloch, lord of human sacrifice; and his Belial, the personification of evil) – in short, to the sawmill, the microcosm of psychopathic capitalism in his village (24). By the time I met Nowlan, however, he was favouring a less romantic view of the working class – indeed, of humanity. He had become the narrative realist who knows that the Egyptians can "hear" his humility – as his reading has allowed him to hear them through their myths – in the buzz of the ancient plague of the poor: the housefly. So the final answer to my request for his prediction about his future in the *Amethyst* interview reprinted here, not surprisingly, is phrased in working class terms:

> I love it when somebody writes that I am one of Canada's most promising poets, likely to be a dominant figure in the next two decades, on the verge of an artistic undertaking of great magnitude, all that sort of thing. But a wicked little part of me asks: if I'm as good as all that why don't some of these people try to get me [a university job] . . . My father who is also a very practical man, but more bitter than I am, used to say that talk is cheap but it takes money to buy rum. I feel like that sometimes.

A primary school dropout's wish for a university appointment is not as audacious as it seems. Five years after my interview with him Nowlan is appointed Writer-in-Residence at the University of New Brunswick, a position he held for the last fifteen years of his life.

Nearly forty years after my interview with him a poet from River Falls, Wisconsin, will focus on this quintessential Alden Nowlan. Thomas R. Smith, in his 2000 "Afterword" (reprinted here) to the second edition of the Nowlan's selected poems in the United States, *What Happened When He Went to the Store for Bread*, states boldly:

> [Nowlan] knows that portraying what is admirable about the underclass without portraying their flaws is worse than a lie – it is a more insidious form of condescension. In this recognition, he has few peers . . . In "What Colour Is Manitoba?" Nowlan jumps fearlessly into his personal experience of class, undeterred by the shame that usually inhibits our attempts to speak of it:

> My family was poor.
> Not disadvantaged curse
> that word of the sniffling
> middle classes, suggesting
> as it does that there's
> nothing worse than
> not being like them.

So Nowlan picked up the verbal gauntlet of class struggle in Canada's perpetual Balkanization of the country in terms of ethnicity, culture, economics, and literary theory. Smith recognizes that the "new world order" propaganda imposed on North America is ruled by economics; and, as Nowlan wrote, "being poor implies some fundamental wrongness of being":

It's as if a chemist
had analyzed a river
and declared that its water
was an inferior form of fire.

The means of production being owned by the ruling class, literary theory tends to bow to the notion
that literature, and therefore its creation in print,
belongs to the educated middle class.

To become a poet out of the underclass and
then to become the writer-in-residence at the
"state" university, nevertheless, intensifies Nowlan's
struggle with the real world. The anxiety and alienation of being found without the security of either
class, while pressured by the demands of both, is
explored by Craig Lawson in his Masters thesis,
"Empty Strength and Throttled Rage: Social Class
Immobility in the Poetry and Prose of Alden
Nowlan." Lawson cites Richard Hoggart, *The Uses
of Literacy* (1957), to focus on Nowlan's aversion to
literary theory: "Working class people are only
rarely interested in movements . . . They are enor-
mously interested in people: they have the novelist's
fascination with individual behaviour, with relationships – though not as to put them into a pattern, but for their own sake" (10). This is consistent
with Nowlan's insistence that he writes for the
same reason his grandmother said she cooked: for
her own amazement.

Whether we are looking at the purgatory of
classless insecurity, or the position of poetry outside

of social class, perhaps the best expression of the poet working in retreat from the world experienced leads to the inevitable conclusion of the expatriate/émigré: "To be a stranger is enough, to be a stranger / in two worlds: that is the ultimate loneliness." All is not angst, of course. Witness the choice for adaptation from the Romanian "Legacy" by Tudor Arghezi, in Nowlan's last volume of poetry, *I Might Not Tell Everybody This* (1982). It reinforces Smith's recognition of Nowlan's class-sub-consciousness in its affirmation of his gift and in its celebration of his hard-earned craft – reminiscent in tone of the sacrificial father figure in the sawmill:

> So that I could change a spade into a pen,
> our ancestors suffered together with their oxen,
> and gathered the sweat of a hundred years to give
>   me ink (56).

Even though the cover of the magazine that published my interview with Nowlan billed him as "A Rising Young Canadian Writer," my questions revealed an attempt to affirm my regional ("Maritime" province) experience as a young writer. When I first met him my subject Alden A. Nowlan, who published extensively in the little magazines of the 1950s in the United States, knew well who he was – some five poetry titles deep of him – including three chapbooks (one in the U.S.), a commercial trade book, and a literary press book of poems. But I had yet to learn of his literary prizes among the American literary magazines, which predicted a great future for him. And I was yet to read his self-assessment made in a letter to the young New Brunswick novelist Raymond Fraser just a year before I met Nowlan: "I am fairly confident that [if] I keep living and growing and developing, I will be considered Canada's greatest living poet by the time I'm 40. But it won't mean anything really." All we can do is write the best we can" (137). This is a highly qualified boast, of course, to a younger writer. But it is also an honest self-fulfilling prophecy.

Shaking off the doctrinaire in all things, Nowlan writes to me, "I believe propaganda of an age is the opposite of what it says it is." Such an opening for any conversation, or a work of art, is a delight to his admirers and a constant burr in the saddle of his detractors – particularly those who seem to need to particularize him in a unique "landscape" or, as I suggest, class-scape. Consequently Nowlan will be dogged during his lifetime by the disparaging connotations of his being labelled a "regionalist," simply because his vast informal education resists any pigeonholing by the formally educated. I argue that Nowlan is simply resisting ruling class bias and its systemic purgatory of sanctioned literary theory.

Canadian poets Patrick Lane and Lorna Crozier begin correcting the regional / class bias in their introduction to the current Canadian volume *Alden Nowlan: Selected Poems*. They write of their high appreciation for the "grace" of Nowlan's voice: "For many years Nowlan was known as a – regional writer,' someone who, because he wrote so intimately about the people and place where he lived, was not considered a writer of first rank. This perception has done a great disservice both to Nowlan and to Canadian poetry." Lane and Crozier recognize that Nowlan's depth of experience and his vulnerability are written from the only universe – "the regions of the heart . . . This is what makes Nowlan great. He has the power to reveal our frailties and our loves, the smallness of our behaviour and the largeness of our spirit" (xviii).

So I have selected here the critics who best help me illustrate Nowlan's resistance to the "regional" label – a critic's mask for class-ism, which I feel hurt him deeply for most of his career. Shades of this – regional boogieman in the theory of Canadian letters lingers even in Nowlan's attempt the year before his death to respond to David Donnell's question in a *Books in Canada* interview about what distinguishes regional literature from folklore: "Well, a folklorist is a purist, what he's making is a kind of museum piece, it's closed off rather than opened up. Whereas a real writer, as opposed to a scholar, say, regards the basic material as living motion, going somewhere, becoming something" (27).

That his work continues "going somewhere," as it transcends the blindness of class stigma, is spoken in volumes by its growing popularity in the United States, thanks to two poets – Nowlan's editor, Thomas R. Smith, and his publisher, Robert Bly. Similarly, British poet and editor Neil Astley of

Bloodaxe Books – owing to common reader requests for more than a recent international anthology offered – released a selected Nowlan in the United Kingdom. *Between Tears and Laughter: Selected Poems* (2004) is Number 1 in a new series called Bloodaxe World Poets.

By the time I met the thirty year-old Nowlan in the summer of 1963, he had been living for eleven years in a single room in a Hartland, New Brunswick. He was about to marry the "peasant" woman he imagined so vividly in verse that she had become real. He published a series of poems to "Therese," beginning with *Under the Ice* (1961). A third in the series appears in *Playing the Jesus Game* (1970), in which

> I tell Therese
> . . . I think it blasphemy
> to write poems
> about pain not experienced (37).

This propriety restates itself most poignantly a decade later in the poem "Bobby Sands," named after the Irish republican who led a prisoners' hunger strike leading to the death of himself and nine others in 1981, but not before he and two other prisoners were elected to Parliament. The action(s) led to the defeat of the British government's attempts to criminalize the republican struggle. Alden writes of Sands:

In common decency, don't speak
of him unless you have gone at least a day
without food, and be sure you understand
that he loved being alive, the same as you (150).

Nowlan's confident, almost father-confessor, sage voice and the "region" of this poem defies provincial and national borders of experience and insight.

In Joseph Brodsky's essay, "The Sound of the Tide," an introduction to a volume of Derek Walcott's poetry the year Alden Nowlan died, Brodsky writes of Walcott being dubbed by detractors and admirers as "a West Indian Poet," or "a black poet from the Caribbean." He finds these definitions "myopic and misleading." And he continues, in the reprint of his collected essays, *Less Than One* (1986), "The mental as well as spiritual cowardice, obvious in these attempts to render this man a regional writer, can be further explained by the unwillingness of the critical profession to admit that the great poet of the English language is a black man" (166). Had he lived to read these words, Alden might have been heard to say, "Amen, Joseph, Amen."

I argue that the regionalizing of Alden Nowlan by Canadian critics was because they were unwilling to admit that a man with a grade four education could be among the country's finest poets. To put it more precisely, because Nowlan wrote in the common language of the working class he was patronized. His ultimate response is found in a file of ideas for poems in his manuscripts at the University of

Calgary and reprinted in the memorial issue of *Pot-tersfield Portfolio*. The language and the concern is that of common humanity:

> When you read
> my poems
> forget the words –
> words mean nothing
> to me –
> What concerns me is
> the unutterable
> loneliness of the
> human heart (12).

Nowlan's professional loneliness is overcome when he engages his first literary friend – poet, professor, and publisher – the late Fred Cogswell. I through correspondence beginning in 1955 and following a face to face meeting in 1961, Fred showers him with support. As Nowlan recounts in "Something to Write About," in *Canadian Literature*, Cogswell "gave me magazines, and books by people like Louis Dudek, Irving Layton and Raymond Souster, through whose work I found my way to people ranging from Catullus to William Carlos Williams" (130).

Then, in 1960, Louis Dudek responded to Nowlan's worry about his lack of formal studies: "Your identity is a greater gift than any education can provide" (135). Nowlan pinned the letter over his desk to sustain him through the writing of his first novel and the pivotal volumes of poems Dudek published, *The Things Which Are* (1962). Subsequently, despite the pressures of post-modern fashion, Nowlan never rides away from his people (his working class roots), as Frank O'Connor in *The Lonely Voice* claims Nowlan's early hero D. H. Lawrence did (143-155).

★

Little more than a decade after my published chat with Nowlan, John Metcalf interviewed him for *Canadian Literature*. Metcalf, the graduate of Beckenham Grammar School for Boys in London, took a mid-Atlantic approach to locating primary school dropout Nowlan in his literary landscape. He asked Nowlan about his writing methods and whether his tradition was British or American. Nowlan declined to identify any conscious imitation of writers who "influenced" him, but he had previously sampled his list of "favourite" writers in a 1969 interview with Robert Cockburn for *The Fiddlehead*: "They keep changing. D. H. Lawrence, William Carlos Williams' Thomas Hardy and Yeats and Norman Mailer; Kenneth Rexroth, I like him – and Irving Layton and Morley Callaghan. Chekhov. And I should mention Ernest Buckler, Raymond Souster – and, oh, Walt Whitman; I still like him. Patrick Kavanagh, too" (11). Nowlan makes eminently clear for Metcalfe, however, that he is Canadian and that his primary influences are Canadian – something his generation is the first to claim.

To Metcalf's probes of his prosody Nowlan

evokes intuition – "non verbal thought." As Nowlan admirers like George Elliot Clarke, George Fetherling, and Robert Bly have remarked on various occasions, of course, the east coast bard works an intelligence and "delicacy of feeling" that seems "self-originated" – as Alan Ginsberg described it in Brian Guns' film. These poets find Nowlan's voice is shaped in the oracular, communal tradition that is as Irish as it is "Maritime" or aboriginal – and that the vernacular voice is as valid as the printed word presumed to be the privileged playground of the formally educated middle class.

In fact, while Nowlan's collecting of books from year one was on a "must read" basis, interviewer Metcalf's most recent outing (*An Aesthetic Underground: A literary Memoir*) opens with a vignette about acquiring books "to *own* them" (2). This approach to library conjures a working class, student writer, Louis Cormier, who met Nowlan in 1967, following a reading by Allen Ginsberg. As Cormier recalls for me in *One Heart, One Way*, "Like these intellectual types he had this living room full of books. So I asked did he really read these books, or were they just for show. He laughed his head off when he heard that" (184-185).

Respecting Metcalf's questions of verse form, line break, and intention, Nowlan has yet to articulate the answer he will give Lesley Choyce nearly a decade later in the *Pottersfield Portfolio* interview (published posthumously) – that preoccupation with *form* over (or without) *content* in poetry reminds him of the speak of political "spin doctors" (3).

Realism transcends Metcalf's queries about Nowlan's relative sentimentality, which is at the heart of Nowlan's work, as he tells David Donnell for *Books in Canada*: "One of the first poems that I was ever profoundly affected by was Ray Souster's poem, I think it's called 'An Address to the Canadian Poets,' and starts something like, 'Now the taverns are closing and the whores are emerging from the alleys . . .' Harsh but liberating compared to the lack of realism, or regionalism for that matter, that existed in Canadian literature at the time" (27).

Bringing humanity to bear where conventional forms seem to the undiscerning to be absent, Nowlan, as he told Cockburn in the *Fiddlehead* interview earlier, finds that he is handicapped by not having glib answers for interviewers, but he tries to be honest when questioned: "The only questions that annoy me after readings are those that aren't really questions at all: people trying to be impressive who aren't really interested in my work" (12).

*

Poet, reviewer, and "occasional reader" of Nowlan's work Geoffrey Cook provides a pivotal link between Metcalf's probing of "form" and Paul Milton's analysis of the major debates over Nowlan's regionalism / nationalism / universalism. Cook bypasses Metcalf's preoccupation with a/the "form(s)" by accepting that Nowlan was one of the poets "who established a – Canadian voice' in poetry – the dominant form of which is the narrative of everyday life in free verse."

Cook recognizes that "Nowlan's greatness" and his originality are the result of a "wide-ranging dialogue with diverse techniques." The complexity and sophistication of the work is driven by the classical tones played by Nowlan's honesty, love, humility, and – echoing Robert Bly's admiration of Nowlan since the 1960s – by his bravery. Bly introduced Nowlan's first U.S. selected, *Playing the Jesus Game*, with "For Alden Nowlan, With Admiration," in which he explains that the psychic bravery in his work is one of the reasons "I've loved Alden Nowlan's poems for years" (10).

Bly finds in Nowlan an antidote for the malaise of "manufactured optimism" in U.S. literature, as Geoffrey Cook similarly finds Nowlan's "careful and original art" good medicine for Canada's "condescending slotting of artistic achievement" by region. He also anticipates the summary of Nowlan critics made by Paul Milton in his analysis of the artist-hero in the poet's fiction.

*

A recently arrived scholar of Nowlan, Paul Milton has helped me understand my search for a prophet in my own land, inspired by a moment when I was six years old. That was the year my mother read to me from *Maclean's* magazine the prize-winning short story "Penny in the Dust" by novelist Ernest Buckler, who would become the subject of my Master's thesis nearly twenty years later. Two years after interviewing Nowlan, I began interviews with the Nova Scotia author of *The Mountain and the Valley* (1952). Milton shows how the Kunstlerromans of Nowlan and his Annapolis Valley antecedent intersect. Milton finds Nowlan's second (and last) novel, *Various Persons Named Kevin O'Brien* (1973), is a response to his critics, including those who rate him by his region.

Milton provides an excellent synopsis of these critics, as he follows the fiction writer-hero Kevin O'Brien on his journey to confront simultaneously his alienation from, and his attraction to, his home place. Milton argues, of course, that language is the key to the journey:

> [Kevin] is the privileged observer constructed by the various languages he speaks: the language of the region, the language of the metropolis and, what constitutes the unifying thread, the language of mass media and pop culture. These three languages correspond roughly to the three positions within the critical discourse surrounding his work . . . As representative of the mainstream press and centralist ideology, Kevin [O'Brien] is implicated in the subordination of the region.

Once again Nowlan defines the space of his own place in literature by reflecting on his short fiction during the intersection between his two novels. He wrote to me, placing his works in a North Ameri-

can region (that I call class) context as he finishes
reading the proofs for *Miracle at Indian River*. "Off
hand the only North American writers I can think
of who have come from a background of rural
poverty and gone onto write about it have been
Negroes. Richard Wright, for instance" (201).

Thomas R. Smith writes in his "Afterword" to
the second U.S. edition of *What Happened When He
Went to the Store for Bread* (2000):

> Since writing the 1993 introduction, I've realized that one
> of the things speaking to me most forcefully in Nowlan's
> work has been his enormous bravery and truthfulness in
> confronting the reality of class, a subject that most Ameri-
> can poets – especially today when many succumb to the
> trend to reinstate poetry to its mid-century status as an
> accoutrement of the privileged life – studiously avoid. In
> this afterword I would like to address more fully Alden
> Nowlan's awareness of class and his refusal to ignore the
> poor.

Smith identifies Nowlan through his empathy with
the working class, while escaping "the class prejudice
by which many liberal, college-educated whites claim
tacit superiority over persons who do the actual physical work of maintaining society." Smith's approach is
quintessential, because it transcends the preoccupation
with definitions of what is parochial, provincial,
regional, or universal. It recognizes that those who
approach literature with a sense of "ownership" write
these definitions. They perpetuate in Canada what I
call the Balkanization of the nation, and they patron-
ize the working poet, such as Alden Nowlan.

To define Nowlan's "job" as a poet, I return to his last book of poems – its title taken from one of his favourite Walt Whitman lines, *I might not tell everybody this* – and, I am looking once again at "Legacy," the adaptation from the Romanian opens: "All that I'll leave you when I die is a name in a book." It is a book "won by slaves and serfs who strained beneath their loads; / sacks filled with their own bones, handed down to me" (56). Nowlan's choice of this poem – while he was offering others to several Canadian poets for adaptation – is not surprising. It embodies Smith's call for an examination of the class-scape in contemporary literary criticism:

> However soft her bed may be when she reads it,
> the Princess will suffer in my book;
> for words of fire and steel are mingled with the soft
>   whisper
> in the book that a slave wrote and the lord reads
> without knowing that in its depths there lies all the rage
>   of my forefathers (57).

Or, as Smith puts it:

> One would be naive, in the present climate of affectless, theory-dominated writing promoted by postmodern English departments, to expect academic critics to look up from their Jorie Grahams and John Ashberys long enough to notice a plain-spoken Maritimer who eschews abstraction and aims for the heart. Yet Nowlan now enjoys, at the very least, a vigorous underground reputation in the U.S. . . . When readers tire, as they inevitably must, of our period's gentrification and numbness, Alden Nowlan's fully human poems will still be there for them.

★

Novelist David Adams Richards finds Nowlan's humanity (what I will call inscape) is the universal in his work, as well as in the faces of those to whom he has recited Nowlan's poems on three continents, as he writes in the *Globe and Mail* twenty years after Nowlan's death:

> I would quote his poems and watch in Sydney, Australia, or Brisbane, or Virginia, or New Orleans, or London, peoples' faces light up for the first time at the man's genius . . . recognize themselves in him, and hear in his simple, straightforward words some great eternal wisdom. It was a wisdom tinged with sorrow that always came, it seemed, in the form of a parting between friends said at the door on a cold winter evening.

Richards, as admirer and friend, listened to Nowlan compare himself to the great writers whom he respected. And he reminded David of others, who like Nowlan had done more than their "share of suffering, though he almost never complained and, like James Joyce, had a resolute will to forge out of the smithy of his soul his own destiny. There is something great in that attribute, that rare ability to be one's own man, and to (as Chekhov said) squeeze the slave from my soul.'"

In his adult life Nowlan compensated for his lonely youth by surrounding himself with the young and old. Richards writes: "As Gorky said of Tolstoy, so someone might have said of Nowlan: 'As long as this man lives no one will be an orphan'."

The young sought him out, as the young must have sought out Emerson, or Socrates. Why? It is simple. The young have to." As one of the young writers who read and listened to Nowlan, the "monologist," Richards evokes in his memoir-essay the sense of why so many of us shared poems and conversation with Nowlan in what he and his wife Claudine created as a "safe house" in the capital city of Fredericton on the edge of the University of New Brunswick campus:

> Some his own age, especially from the university, were wary of him because, just like Beethoven with the nobility, he could not bow easily to those who had not come to knowledge within the harsh life-and-death parameters he himself has faced. But the young came. He never so much instructed them, but listened to them. Perhaps, who knows, they were taken seriously for the very first time in their lives.

*

So I have invited these five younger writers – three who, like myself, were taken very seriously by Nowlan and two who never met him, but who take his works very seriously – to help me explain why I had no reservations when Robert Bly – who has translated and/or published more than twenty international poets in the United States – wrote in his foreword to my biography of my old friend (as well as a friend of John, David, and Geoffrey): "Alden Nowlan is the greatest Canadian poet of the twentieth century."

1 May 2005

WORKS CITED

Unless otherwise indicated, all of the citations of Nowlan's poems are referenced from: *Alden Nowlan: Selected Poems.* eds. Patrick Lane and Lorna Crozier. Toronto: Anansi, 1996. All other page (or date) references (as with Nowlan's journal-published statements) are to the volume immediately preceding the citation, as in: "Afterword to Genesis," *The Mysterious Naked Man.* Toronto: Clarke, Irwin, 1969. Alden Nowlan's letters to the editor of these essays are found in their originals in the Papers of Gregory M. Cook at Dalhousie University Archives, Killam Library, Halifax, and their copies are found in The Alden Nowlan Papers at the Special Manuscript Collections, University of Calgary Library, Calgary. They are referenced here when applicable, as quoted in: Gregory M. Cook. *One Heart, One Way / Alden Nowlan: a writer's life.* Lawrencetown Beach, N.S.: Pottersfield Press, 2003. (Otherwise the box, file and folio numbers are referenced as found in: Moore, Jean M., Compiler; Apollonia Steele and Jean F. Tuner, Eds. *The Alden Nowlan Papers*, University of Calgary Press (Calgary: 1992).

Nowlan, Alden. "Alden Nowlan Reports," Saint John: *The Telegraph-Journal*, 7 May 1969.

Nowlan, Alden. "My father is dying . . ." typescript [iii], Nowlan Collection, Harriet Irving Library, University of New Brunswick, Fredericton, New Brunswick.

Nowlan, Alden. "At the Mill," *Amethyst.* 2:4 Summer (1963): 24.

Lawson, Craig. "Empty Strength and Throttled Rage: Social Class Immobility in the Poetry and Prose of Alden Nowlan." Master Thesis, University of Calgary, 2000.

Nowlan, Alden. *I Might Not Tell Everybody This.* Toronto: Clarke, Irwin, 1982.

Donnell, David. An Interview with Alden Nowlan. *Books in Canada.* June/July (1982): 26-28.

Astley, Neil. ed. *Staying Alive: Real Poems for Unreal Times.* Bloodaxe Books, 2002 / New York: Miramax, 2003.

Nowlan, Alden. *Playing the Jesus Game.* Trumansburg, NY: New Books, 1970.

Brodsky, Joseph. *Less Than One.* Toronto: Collins Publishers, 1988.

O'Connor, Frank. *The Lonely Voice: a study of the short story*. Cleveland: World Publishing Co., 1963.

Metcalf, John. *An Aesthetic Underground: A literary Memoir*. Toronto: Thomas Allen Publishers, 2003.

Cockburn, Robert. "An Interview with Alden Nowlan," in "The Alden Nowlan Special Issue." *Fiddlehead*. 81 (1969): 5-13.

Choyce, Lesley. "Introduction" [Memorial] to "Alden Nowlan Interview," *Pottersfield Portfolio* 5 (1983): 2-3.

Nowlan, Alden. *Playing the Jesus Game*. Trumansburg, N.Y.: 1970.

Buckler, Ernest. 'Penny in the Dust,' *The Rebellion of Young David and Other Stories*, Selected by Robert D. Chambers, Toronto: McClelland and Stewart Limited: Toronto, 1975, 3-7.

Nowlan, Alden. "Poet in Hiding," *Nomad* 5-6 (1960), 50-52, Nowlan Collection, Harriet Irving Library, University of New Brunswick, Fredericton.

Alden Nowlan: A Rising Young Canadian Writer Talks to *Amethyst*

AN INTERVIEW WITH GREGORY M. COOK

EDITOR: How did you start writing, Alden, and what motivates you to write?

NOWLAN: Now, that is one of those very simple questions that requires a very complicated answer. I started writing when I was eleven years old, and, obviously, there have been enormous changes in my motivations in the nineteen years since then. I began to think of myself seriously as a writer when I was about twenty-five. No, I didn't start thinking of myself seriously then, but I started taking the writing – the work – seriously which is a very different thing. Since then the things which motivate me to write have developed a great deal: my attitude toward writing today is different from what it was a year ago, for instance.

ED: This is probably true of many professions?

N: Yes, and in retrospect sometimes you find that what you felt motivated you at some particular time in the past wasn't the real motivation at all. Anyway, I don't ask myself about motivations very often.

ED: What influenced you to write when you were eleven?

N: Oh, I lived in the backwoods of Nova Scotia, you
know: I had a nineteenth century frontier kind
of childhood, in a sense. We were poor and isolated and I was alone a lot – like Huckleberry
Finn, you know, not the Huck Finn that got his
picture on sentimental calendars but the Huck
Finn in Mark Twain's book, a beautiful, horrible
book – and I was steeped in the *Bible*, saturated
in a kind of Calvinist Baptist, almost Jewish the-
ology, and when I was ten or so I thought of
myself as kind of an apprentice prophet: I was
going to be like Isaiah when I grew up, I guess.
I even thought I had visions. That kind of thing.
And I started writing them down because Isaiah
and Jeremiah and all those old fellows wrote
their visions down. The Words that the Lord
spake Unto His Servant, Alden, that kind of
thing, you know. And, of course, I wanted recognition for my ego –

ED: Why would a fellow from the backwoods get an
idea he could receive recognition by writing?
Couldn't he get recognition for anything else?

N: You can look at this in so many ways that it is
very difficult to express it simply and honestly.
When I was eleven I saw this move about Jack
London, a very bad movie. But, you know, it
showed how he'd come from a background
something like the background that I came from
– a very poor and a very hard environment – and
then he'd written books and things and, by the
time the movie was over, you know, he was a

celebrity and a millionaire and all that kind of thing. Well, of course, when I was eleven I wanted to be a celebrity and a millionaire. When you're poor, you know, when you're a kid what hurts you isn't the lack of material things. Usually you don't even realize you're poor, in that sense. But we all of us want some kind of recognition as human beings – putting it this way it sounds trite and silly but I can't think of any other way of putting it at the moment – and that kind of recognition is damned hard to get when you're poor, really dirt poor. I mean a kid doesn't care if his father is earning thirty dollars a month as my father was when I was a kid. But he cares desperately if he thinks he doesn't matter. I suppose that being a prophet and being a writer helped convince me that I mattered. Really, I started writing as some kids start stealing hub caps. I don't mean to make a big thing of this, because it isn't a central thing in my consciousness, but I am the first serious writer – I don't know how seriously I dare think of myself as a writer – who has spring from the old Anglo-Saxon–Celtic rural proletariat in Canada. I mean if I were a character in a Faulkner novel I suppose I'd have to be Snopes rather than Sartotius.

ED: Why do you hesitate to think of yourself seriously as a writer?

N: I suppose it's something like Robert Frost saying that he didn't call himself a poet because that was a title other people conferred on you.

ED: I guess it is a well-remembered quotation from his CBC interview.

N: Of course, I don't want to exaggerate this. I don't like to be portrayed as a primitive writer. I don't think of myself that way at all.

ED: I recall a suggestion that you were a primitive writer and that you made your poems of the trivial and insignificant things. Is this because the reviewer has probably been brought up in a different mainstream of life and to him Maritime people and the life you write about is primitive?

N: I don't know that the life of a New Brunswick farmer is much more primitive than the life of a bar tender in Toronto. It's mostly that these people who tend to think of the subjects of my poems as primitive and violent think of any kind of real life as primitive and violent – I mean any kind of real life outside of a certain, oh, suburban, sophisticated, academic kind of real life. I mean Eli Mandel wrote a very kind and good review of one my books in *The Canadian Forum*. And in it he said something like this: "Mr. Nowlan's world of child beatings, barn burnings and Saturday night dances isn't the real Maritimes . . ." Well, that is like saying my whole life has been a figment of my own imagination.

ED: Yes, with what authority did he make such a judgment? The people you portray are Maritime people, I would say, Alden, being a Maritimer myself. Do you start with people rather than ideas?

N: Well, of course, I'm much more concerned with ideas in my recent work. But if we're going to write simply about ideas, I'd do philosophical essays instead of poems.

ED: Probably we would find the answer to this question by reading a good cross section of your work, but driving up today I asked myself, how would you describe these Maritime people: what kind of people are they?

N: Well, of course, people are affected by the place in which they live – societies of people as well as individuals. Obviously, the fish merchants in St. John's, for example, are a different kind of people from the pulp cutters in Hants County, Nova Scotia. And both groups have some distinctly Maritime outlooks that differentiate them from people in Nebraska or California or Quebec. Here we have the old Family Compact, you know, and we have the old red neck and cracker families too, some of whom have lived in the same parish since 1780. There isn't the mobility that that there is in most of America. But, Lord, I don't write about Maritime people in capital letters, as if they were some special species. I have certain feelings, certain responses – I could well have these same feelings and responses if I lived in Montreal, but I'd write them in a different way, simply because I'd have different experiences and see different things if I lived in Montreal. You remember what Faulkner said about all he knew was a little bunch of farmers down around Oxford, Mississippi, so that's what he wrote about? Well, he could say that about himself, but he'd raise hell if anyone else has said it.

ED: I know your first novel is under consideration for publication; will this first major work, when we read it, deal with these real Maritime people?

N: Everything I write deals with what it is like to be Alden Nowlan, because that is the only thing I know about. But, yes, I suppose the people in the book will be real Maritime people. Anyway, they are all real, and they all lived in the Maritimes.

ED: Do you feel that "Love Letter" is a Maritime story, Alden?

N: The girl in the story is living in the Maritimes, I guess. But, Lord, there are people like her in Peking, aren't there, I mean? Look, the popular fiction nowadays mostly deals with sophisticated suburbanites, the lives of sophisticate suburbanites. But the percentage of sophisticated suburbanites in the world is pretty damn small. *Franny and Zooy*, for instance. I'm a Salinger man, myself. But *Franny and Zooy*, I mean taking just the details of their lives, could anything be more provincial, really? If we were to assess these things on a purely satisfactory basis "Love Letter" would be less provincial or regional or whatever you want to call it than *Franny and Zooy*.

ED: To become less universal and too provincial is dangerous.

N: Oh, yes. And I feel my work is less and less provincial because I myself am becoming less and less provincial. I mean a lot of my stuff has probably been provincial or parochial, but that isn't a failure in the material, it is a failure in me. I can write a lot better now than I wrote when I did the poems in *Under the Ice* [1961]. I'm ready to fight anyone who says that *The Things Which Are* [1962] is a book of regional verse. No, I'm not ready to fight them. Really, I care less and less about what people say about my poems and stories. No, that is false too, in a way, because I'm sensitive to praise and dispraise, but I don't let it affect my writing.

ED: A common idea among many people is that a writer has certain beefs – that he is sensitive to things happening around him. What things are you sensitive to now? What are your beefs?

N: Oh, I don't like hypocrisy, and I don't like fakes – I think the important division in the world is between the people who are real and the people who are fakes.

ED: And do you find this just in Maritime people or in people wherever you meet them?

N: Oh, this is universal – like the damned and the elect, I guess. I mean I think people are damned to a degree to which they are fakes. Christ, according to the New Testament – the only thing that made him angry was hypocrisy. I'm putting this very badly, but this is a very strong concept with me.

ED: Are there any people you have encounter in life that you feel have affected your work?

N: Oh, there have been a few people that I've loved very deeply and of course these people have affected me and, of course, the way in which they have affected me has been reflected in my work. But no teachers or anything like that . . . I mean for years and years when I was a kid I concealed the fact that I wrote, as though it were a secret vice. I was twenty-five years old before I even talked with people who had any interest in writing or poetry or anything like that. I don't suppose there is a writer in the world who has spent less time talking about writing than I have.

ED: Who among the people you have read do you think have influenced your work?

N: Oh, this is very difficult to answer too. I mean I admire certain writers who have had little influence on my work. Little apparent influence. I began to write before I'd read very much, you see.

ED: Was this good for your work?

N: I don't think it was good for me, in the technical sense, but it was probably good for me; if I had known, without having any formal education – if I had been aware of the complexities of writing, I might have been so discouraged at the beginning, it would have seemed so hopeless, that I might have given it up, don't you see. I sort of grew up into it. By the time I knew how serious it all was I was in too deep to get out.

ED: Do you want to get out now?

N: Oh, when you've been thinking about something every day since you were eleven years old – it is something like, you know, a kid thinking at eleven that he has a vocation for the priesthood, and he keeps thinking of it through adolescence, that kind of thing is pretty common, and, well, after a while, it is just part of you, like having blue eyes. You don't think about it any more. It just is. That's why it is hard for me to discuss motivations and that kind of thing.

ED: Why do you choose at one time, Alden, to write a poem and at another time to write a story?

N: Oh, probably in my earlier work there were times when I did things in poems I should have done in short stories. But, for me, the big difference is that in order to write a short story I have to be removed to a certain degree from the thing about which I'm writing and I need more time and freedom. More objectively. I mean I could imagine someone deciding to commit suicide and writing a poem about it and then killing himself but I can't imagine anyone contemplating suicide writing a short story about it.

ED: Also I find there is a time element involved; there are moments when I have strong feelings but have only time to concentrate to the length of a poem.

N: Yes, it's a physical thing, too. When you have to earn a living by doing something else, you have very little time for writing. Most of the stories I've done that were any good I did when I had the Canada Council thing ["fellowship" / grant] and had whole days in which to write. This purely materialistic aspect of writing interests me in some ways more than talking about techniques and influences and that kind of thing. I mean I remember reading where Sinclair Lewis spoke at a student writers' conference and they asked him what was the best advice he'd ever had about writing and he said the discovery that had helped him most was that putting band aids on his index fingers kept him from getting cuticles when he was typing. I think maybe it would be better if writers talking to one another talked more about that kind of thing. The important stuff you have to work out for yourself.

ED: Do you have any major work brewing now, Alden – a collection of your short stories or more poems?

N: Oh, by this time next year I'd like to have another collection of verses ready – something better than anything I've done – and maybe a collection of stories: I'd like to have enough stories to make a book, although I don't know that I'll ever be a really good story writer. This next collection of verses will be better organized. Two or three central themes.

ED: I think it was also Robert Frost who said, "The most precious quality of a poem will remain in its having run itself and carried away the poet with it". Is this true of your own experience?

N: Oh, yes. When you bring it down to the ultimate thing, I write poetry for the emotional release of it. It's the same as being in love with a girl. I mean sometimes there's a moment when you've finished the poem – even if you decide later that it is a bad poem – I mean the quality of a poem as a poem I don't think has anything to do with this: I've had the feeling strongly after doing a poem I later decided was a failure, you know. The feeling of triumph and, of, yes, power, the feeling that you can cope with anything and the wonderful feeling of release. I think that is true, if that is what Frost was talking about.

ED: Personal satisfaction is perhaps the greatest benefit you get from your work.

N: Oh, yes. Otherwise it wouldn't be worth doing, would it?

ED: The first poem in Irving Layton's latest books, *Balls for a One-Armed Juggler*, called "There Were No Signs" seems to say at the very out start – no matter how comic Layton appears to some – that Layton's poetry is a therapy for Layton. In the course of his work this particular poet seems to become better acquainted with himself first and therefore humanity.

N. Yes, that's very true. And sometimes I find meanings in my own work after it's done that I wasn't altogether conscious of at the time that I wrote. A quotation too that I like is D. H. Lawrence's, that my motto is "Art for my sake." I think that contains a great deal of truth.

ED: I think it was a poet we both know [Fred Cogswell] who wrote me that for him it had been much too happy a year for creativity, but this attitude often implies that the creative person works from an unhappy state of mind.

N: There's an extent to which that is true. I can't conceive of any completely happy person, if there was such a person anyway, being a writer – especially a poet. I think that you must have certain reservoirs of unhappiness and often you can write some very beautiful things out of unhappiness. Most of the people in the world are unhappy really and you're saying something that people will feel.

But there does come a point, I feel, of actual depression in which you get the feeling that all poetry is bunk anyway. I've had moods when I've felt that. There's a feeling that you might have as a serious writer, at the beginning of your career, that you don't really have what it takes; no matter how much you want to do this, there's some lack in you. That is a very deadening feeling. But far worse than that is the feeling that occasionally may come over you that none of it matters.

The feeling not expressed in quite this same way is found in Marianne Moore's poem, "I too dislike it." There is the feeling that even poets dislike poetry, but when you come to the state of depression that you doubt the value of writing – I imagine all serious writers have that feeling – I don't think any productivity can come out of that. There's a certain degree of unhappiness that you can write out of, but when your unhappiness reaches the point of frustration, I don't think any writing can come out of it.

ED: Any type of therapy on oneself is sometimes a painful thing. I should think that this might make the writer unhappy – to reveal himself.

N: And possibly I have that feeling particularly strong, coming from my background – we as a group in the Maritimes tend to be an inarticulate and inhibited people. I mean, you can't conceive of us talking with one another like people talk in Dostoyevsky's novels. There is a great inhibition to be overcome, but I feel that any writing to be worthwhile at all has to be something you feel very intimately, and very deeply. Often you'll hesitate to express these things because – I think this is again a quotation from Lawrence after he had written *Sons and Lovers* he wrote to one of his friends and said, "I feel that I have thrown something holy before the asses, apes and dogs." You get this feeling that you exposed yourself, you know.

ED: Do you find that sometimes under emotional stress you are prompted to write? For example, if my wife was away for a couple of weeks, I would find something missing that seems to compel me to write.

N: Yes, I think this is very true.

ED: You are a single man yourself, but you can probably think of something similar.

N: Any crisis in your life is certainly to be reflected in your work.

ED: I gather from the very strong feeling expressed in your recent poem in *Canadian Forum* on your father ["At the Mill"] that he is a person whose movements affect you very much.

N: Oh, I suppose we're all deeply affected by our parents. It's just that if you're a poet you write it down.

ED: As I mentioned you are a single man now. You're news editor of the *Hartland Observer*; you were quite involved in your regular writing; do you have any idea now of a future for yourself?

N: Well, I'd certainly like to get a job that would give me a decent living and leave me sufficient time and energy to devote to my writing. I'm a very practical person – I think most poets are intensely practical people. I love it when somebody writes that I am one of Canada's most promising poets, likely to be a dominant figure in the next two decades, on the verge of an artistic undertaking of great magnitude, all that sort of thing. But a wicked little part of me asks: if I'm as good as all that why don't some of these people try to get me something like, oh, say, a position as a lecturer in poetry where I'd make enough money to get married and still have a little time in which to write poems and stories. My father who is also a very practical man, but more bitter than I am, used to say that talk is cheap but it takes money to buy rum. I feel like that sometimes.

16 June 1963

Alden Nowlan

INTERVIEWED BY JOHN METCALF

METCALF: What are your working methods? How
much rewriting do you do?

NOWLAN: Well, almost everything I write goes
through two phases. Usually I do the first version
of a poem almost as an exercise in free associa-
tion except that it's tethered to the point that
brought it into being. Sometimes I think of these
first versions as first drafts and sometimes I think
of them as notes toward a poem. Some of them
never go beyond this phase. The rest I throw into
drawer and periodically I dig through a bunch of
them and pick out those that appeal to me at the
moment and them I work at them as objectively and coldly as possible, almost as if they were
somebody else's work. Then when I'm preparing
the manuscript for a collection of poems I make
further changes in almost every poem that goes
into the book, not to make them conform to any
theoretical principles but according to Robert
Graves' dictum that a poet ought to handle his
lines and images and words like a housewife sep-
arating the good tomatoes from those that are
under-ripe or spoiled.

METCALF: What have been the main poetic influences in your career? To what tradition do you
feel you belong – the British or the American?

NOWLAN: I think perhaps I belong to the first generation of Canadian poets to be influenced most by other Canadian poets or maybe I should have said: to be influenced most directly by other Canadian poets. I believe Margaret Atwood says her most important influences are Canadian. None of the older Canadian poets could have said that. Every previous generation turned to England or the United States for models. And as for the younger Canadian poets I doubt if any of them could even name one of their English or American contemporaries. The more I think about it, John, the more I feel that this question is ten years out of date.

METCALF: Have there been any particular poets who have influenced you?

NOWLAN: Oh, there have been dozens and dozens of poets that have influenced me either a little or a great deal at various periods. I've been writing poems and stories ever since ever since I was eleven years old. It would be easy for me to declare that I didn't begin to write seriously until I was twenty-five and then mention some of the poets I happened to be reading when I was that age as being major influences – but that would be essentially false. One of the important influences on me when I got to be reasonably mature, say seventeen or eighteen years old, was D.H. Lawrence. And it's curious. I think someone reading my work would be very unlikely to find echoes of Lawrence but only recently I was intrigued to discover that Lawrence also had a great influence on Orwell. And reading Orwell you wouldn't guess that Lawrence had any influence on him at all. Lawrence was much more of a romantic than Orwell was or than I am, and so if all three of us were using the same instrument we'd none of us be playing the same tune. Quite often people look at a writer and glibly reel off a list of the people that he resembles who lived prior to his time and say that they were his influences. I've had reviewers say that of course I was influenced by so and so – and it was somebody I'd never read beyond a few things in an anthology perhaps.

METCALF: I remember your saying to me once that Robinson was a great influence.

NOWLAN: Yes, Robinson was a big influence on me when I was about twenty-five – but I'd come to him through Fred Cogswell, you see, just as I came to the Black Mountain people through Layton and Souster.

METCALF: From your early books to your latest there's been a progressive loosening of form – abandoning of metre and rhyme.

NOWLAN: That's come about through an almost purely intuitive process. At intervals over the years I've looked back over my work of, say, the previous six months and I've suddenly realized that I've been writing differently. The important thing to keep in mind about the process of development as it applies to me is that my whole intellectual life, the whole growth of my mind, for the first twenty-five years of my life took place in a solitude that couldn't have been greater if I had been living alone on an island. That's so odd that people find it impossible to understand – they think they understand, but they don't. Because it wasn't necessary for me to verbalize any of the reactions that I was having or to justify any direction that I was taking – because there was absolutely nobody at all for me to talk with about such things, many of these processes remain on the non-verbal level that we call intuition. I think that's what intuition is: non-verbal thought.

METCALF: What's been the influence of Olsen and Creeley and Duncan? Had they anything to do with your formal development?

NOWLAN: Oh, yes, very much so. You see that just as I went from Cogswell who had influenced me directly to Robinson who had influenced him directly, so I went from Layton and Souster and Dudek to their direct influences, which included either Creeley, Olson or Duncan or people, such as Williams, who had influenced Creeley, Olsen and Duncan. There was Kenneth Fearing, for instance, who must have had an enormous influence on Souster. And I like Kenneth Patchen – but I could never write like that. I think it's important to find the influences, the influences that are sufficiently congenial to be useful. There was a time when like everyone else

in those days I read and re-read Dylan Thomas,
but it would have been fatal for me to have
developed a Dylan Thomas kind of style – simply because we're such different people. You have
to begin with your basic nature. There are certain facets to my mind and my manner of
expressing myself that are as inescapable as the
fact that I'm six feet three inches tall and have
blue-grey eyes. And that's true of everyone. I've
also been influenced by the Irishman Patrick
Kavanaugh. But none of this conflicts with my
earlier statement that my most direct influences
were Canadian. I came to English and American
poetry later.

METCALF: You have written a poem on the death
of William Carlos Williams and I wonder if you'd
studied any of his or Olson's theoretical writings
on poetry.

NOWLAN: Yes, I've read Olson's projective verse
essay that old Williams liked so well that he
included it in his autobiography, and I've read a
lot of Williams' critical pieces. But I've always
had the suspicion that with Williams at least the
criticism was only a kind of unwilling justifica-
tion for the work, that he only bothered putting
that kind of thing down on paper because he felt
that he had to do it in order to obtain critical
respectability for his work and work like it.
Bertrand Russell said that every philosopher
ought first publish a book written in jargon that
no layman could understand, and once having

done that he wouldn't have to bother with such jargon any more. And perhaps a poet ought to begin by publishing a book of criticism with all sorts of high-sounding phrases – adumbrate is a very big word with the critics – and then he wouldn't be expected to waste any more time with that sort of thing, he could simply write poems, which is what a poet ought to be doing. But I think Pound's critical writings are invaluable – I keep recommending them to students. I wrote to old Pound when he was in St. Elizabeth's Hospital and he sent me a note saying, "I tray-sure yer replies," whatever that meant.

On this continent and in our lifetime it seems that to justify yourself as a writer you must first proclaim critical theory and then proceed to demonstrate it. If Shakespeare had been required to do that he'd have spent his whole life in some obscure place writing a critique on literature that nobody would remember and he'd never have found time to write any of his plays. But, of course, Shakespeare, as they liked to point out in the 18th century, wasn't an intellectual. He broke all the rules. He's been stuffed and mounted for so long that we tend to forget that. One thing that I've come to feel more and more strongly is that because so many North American poets are professors there's come to be a confusion of roles. Take the questions after a poetry reading – I find that ninety percent of those questions are questions you'd ask a professor, not questions you'd ask a poet. Now, if it happened that I was a professor as well as a poet I'd slip automatically out of my poet's laurel wreath and into my academic gown and answer as a professor without even being conscious of changing from one role to another. If most of the poets were motor mechanics there would be the same confusion of roles, I suppose, and during the question period after a reading people would say, "Mr. Layton, I'm having transmission trouble. What should I do about it?" [Milton] Acorn, [Al] Purdy, myself, and [John] Newlove, are about the only Canadian poets on my generation that aren't also professors.

METCALF: I'd like to ask you another question about form − about the line divisions in your work. Are they sense units, breath units or purely typographical?

NOWLAN: They many different things but above all they're attempts to find a typographical substitute for the purely visual and oral things that play such an important part in a conversation − facial expression, gestures of the hands, intonations of the voice. I might end a line in a certain way in an attempt to create the typographical equivalent of a shrug, for instance. Then, too, some of the divisions are intended to make the reader slow down − to read certain words in units of five instead of ten, for instance. And sometimes the break adds an additional level of meaning in that the reader is led to believe that

I'm saying one thing and then an instant later he finds that I'm saying something else which doesn't supersede the first thing, but amplifies it, or modifies it. The thing that he thought I was going to say and the thing that I did say are both there, one strengthening and supporting the other. There's a deliberate instant of ambiguity, you see, which reflects the ambiguity of life.

Now, I have no intention of giving you specific examples – of pointing out how that works or is intended to work in individual poems. That would be like a pitcher walking in before the pitch to tell the batter what kind of a ball he was going to throw at him. Somewhere years ago, I forget where, I read the objective of the poet, like the objective of the pitcher in baseball, is to make the batter understand – too late. I was immediately struck by the truth of that.

METCALF: When you give public readings, enjambment often doesn't follow the printed text of the poem.

NOWLAN: Right. The dominant tradition in poetry written in English has always been that poetry is heightened conversation, an oral art. But the people who carry the Black Mountain theories to their ultimate extreme – they seem to forget that fully literate people don't move their lips when they read. And they also forget that the eye takes in as many as, oh, say, twenty-five words at a glance – whereas when you're listening to somebody reading aloud you hear the words,

one by one, in succession. The line divisions on
the printed page are for the reader – but if I'm
there in the flesh and come to a point on the
printed page I used a certain line divisions to
indicate a shrug – well, I simply shrug. Mark
Twain when he was reading his stories in public
didn't *read* them at all, he simply *told* the same
story. Then there's also the fact that I'm not an
actor. I don't have the dramatic ability to indicate
verbally the equivalent of, say, a semi-colon, and
so possibly I insert another word – an extra word
that a professional actor might not need to use.
Some of my poems now have one printed and
one spoken version. Sometimes I change entire
lines in them when I read them before an audience. At first I worried about that and I used to
feel that I ought to make the printed poem conform to the spoken poem, the poem as spoken
by me, and I'd rewrite them – but I found it
weakened them on the page. Now you take
someone like Allen Ginsberg who is constantly
reading to large audiences. Now when he writes
a poem he knows that he's going to read it in an
auditorium and there are going to be an enormous number of distractions there – such as
light-bulbs breaking and doors slamming, people
coughing, and of course people will be thinking
about other things, wondering if their wives are
being unfaithful, if they can pay the rent, worry-
ing about the pimple on their earlobe. Now if
you were reading the book you could close it

and go back to it later. You can't do that at a reading and so to express something you need only hint at on the page you may have to repeat the same word or line several times.

METCALF: So, if the poet writes with a live audience in mind he writes less purely than he would were he writing for the eye of the reader.

NOWLAN: Oh, yes. You see I don't write poems for an audience. An audience is a crowd. I write poems for one person at a time. I distrust the kind of thing that can be shouted to a crowd. At the end of the road I see the spellbinding orator. I'd rather talk with one person that speechify to a thousand.

METCALF: Your poems seem to split into two major divisions – poems that are descriptive or lyric (and some of the descriptive poems become poems of total metaphor) and then there are discursive or philosophical poems. There's a third, smaller group of satiric poems. The descriptive and lyric poems seem to belong to the earlier books in general. And the discursive, philosophic and satiric poems [seem] to be increasing in your later books [Nowlan's most recent being *I'm a Stranger Here Myself,* 1974].

NOWLAN: Well, I suppose I'm what Neruda would call an impure poet, in the sense that I feel that almost anything that can be experienced can be turned into poetry – and I suppose that most of us tend to become more philosophical, if that's the right word, as we get older. Possibly one reason why I now publish more poems of ideas is that earlier on I didn't have sufficient experience and it didn't come off, I mean that the poems of that kind that I attempted didn't come off. As for the satires, well, Bernard Shaw said that if you told people the truth you'd be well advised to make them laugh, because then they'd be less apt to kill you. But mostly I think of the satires as a type of light verses.

METCALF: You say you didn't have enough experience earlier to write more philosophic poems yet some of the descriptive poems, and certainly those that become total metaphor, are just as sophisticated and possibly even more profound.

NOWLAN: Yes. Yes, I think I may have phrased that very badly. Some of the earlier poems which were articulating ideas were doing so at a non-verbal level – no, what I mean is, a non-abstract level – because that's how my mind was working. It goes back to what I said about working out my ideas in isolation. In those days I *thought* in total metaphor to a greater extent than I do now and so inevitably I wrote in the way I thought. The ideas were expressing themselves not only on the page but in my mind almost wholly through *things*. You know, William Carlos Williams said, "No ideas but in things." You must remember that I was born and grew up in a very primitive society. I suppose in some senses I'm like one of those eighteenth- century Tahitians that were brought to England and thrown among the London literary men. Even when they learned Greek and Latin they couldn't change what they'd been, don't you see?

METCALF: In seemingly simple poems like "Hens" (30) and "Palomino Stallion" (95) they work simultaneously as pure description and pure metaphor. There is a total fusion. Did you see these poems from the start as metaphor or did the fusion come as you were working from the thing seen?

NOWLAN: Well, the thought came from the thing seen and the poem came from the thought that had been provided by the thing seen – and in another and maybe even truer sense it all happened at once. [Pause] There was a time a few years ago when I had this worry, and it was a very real worry at the time, that I had no inventiveness. Not no imagination, but no inventiveness. In other words some people can sit down and invent an incident to illustrate an idea, but I find it almost literally impossible to do that. I'm a born liar, but that's different. Born liars don't invent things, they simply can't bear the unvarnished truth – or I ought to say the naked fact, because there's a great difference between a fact and a truth. I'm sorry to be blathering around so much but I have to keep hesitating to think – which is what prevented [Federal Progressive Conservative Leader Robert] Stanfield from winning the last election. The poor bastard stops to think when he's asked a question and then he looks like an idiot because nobody does that anymore.

METCALF: In some of your later work as the forms have moved further from the traditional, it seems sometimes that the colloquial − that speaking voice you were talking about earlier − falls in to the prosaic.

NOWLAN: It's one of the risks you have to take. To be a writer you have to run the risk of making a fool of yourself. When I run the risk of sounding prosaic I run the risk deliberately − just as I sometimes deliberately run the risk of sounding sentimental. I think you have to risk sentimentality if you're going to write anything that matters because after all sentimentality is very close to the things that *genuinely* move people − it's not a falsity but simply an exaggeration.

METCALF: "Ypres 1915" (63), which you've said is one of your favourites among your work, is a poem that plays on the edge of sentimentality the whole time.

NOWLAN: Sure. That poem is essentially a dialogue between the brain and the guts, the cerebral and the visceral. The tension between the sentimental or the near sentimental and the cynical and the near-cynical is deliberate. Which reminds me that a I wrote a poem called "He Raids the Refrigerator and Reflects Upon Parenthood" (79), and because the emotion that evoked the poem was a maudlin one (for we all of us *do* feel maudlin at one time or another, provided we're human, and to be a poet is to express what humans feel) – I actually began the poem with the words, "Nowlan, you maudlin boob." I feel now that I should have entitled it "A Maudlin Poem," because there was one reviewer who said, "Unfortunately, Mr. Nowlan has one maudlin poem in his book called 'He Raids the Refrigerator.'" And so this particular reviewer didn't know enough to know that the poem was *supposed* to be maudlin even though I'd said so in the poem. But then I don't suppose he'd read the poem. Many reviewers don't.

Any poet who deals with the emotions that move people to tears is going to be accused by some people of being sentimental because sentimentality is by definition an excessive emotion and what to one person may seem excessive to another may seem perfectly normal. Thomas Hardy was also accused of being sentimental. I happen to be a very passionate person who is very readily moved to both tears and laughter and if I denied this I would be false to myself. Now I assume that T. S. Eliot was a very cold person, but he was also a very great poet. That coldness was natural to him, presumably.

But by God! I'd rather have spent an evening with Charles Dickens or Thomas Hardy than with T. S. Eliot.

METCALF: Your poetry is far more visual than oral. Is the musical element in poetry unimportant to you?

NOWLAN: If you mean by "musical element" what I think you mean – the use of pleasant sounds merely for the sake of using pleasant sounds – I try not to put anything into my poems that isn't functional. And, then, too, it's not entirely a matter of choice. I suppose the music that I respond to is very simple, unsophisticated music – the visual equivalent would be Norman Rockwell. In so much criticism and in so much of the pretentious bosh uttered by writers when they're discussing their craft there's the unspoken assumption that everything you do as a writer is the result of choice or in accord with some critical theory. In reality, of course, a poet born tone-deaf is going to be an entirely different poet from a poet born with perfect pitch. You have to work within the limitation of what God made you. A moose might prefer to be a butterfly but he'd be a damned foolish moose if he wasted any time feeling sorry for himself because he wasn't one.

METCALF: *Things*, their physical appearance and texture, dominate a lot of your poetry. Is this a religious position? Do you believe in immanence?

NOWLAN: I have a very strong, almost primitive, sense of the sacredness of objects and things. Animals. Someone once pointed out to me that in all my poems there wasn't a single animal called "it" – they were always "he" or "she." In my poetry I try to tell the truth. It's a losing battle because there are so many truths you can't really tell but I try to show the thing as it *is*. That's the reason why I named one of my early books *The Things Which Are* after St. John the Divine being told by an angel to write "the things which thou hast seen and the things which are." (I think *now* it was a rather bombastic title – but at the same time it was trying to express this devotion to the truth of things.) There is a kind of truth in a beer can, you know. If you say, "There's a beer-can" that's something everyone can establish. They can go and see if it's there. But if you say, "The ineluctable Providence is shining down upon you," you won't know whether it is or not. Yes, I believe in immanence very strongly.

METCALF: Yours is a sophisticated and "high" art, yet I've heard you quoted as saying that you write for truck drivers. Were you drinking that day or just annoyed with someone?

NOWLAN: As I remember, about that truck driver business, I said to someone who later wrote a newspaper thing that *if* there comes a time that truck drivers read poetry, mine will be the poetry they read, and I think that's quite true. I hope that you're right when you call my poetry "sophisticated". I like to think it's *elegant*. But it seems to me that the very greatest literature has all sorts of levels. *Huckleberry Finn*, you know. The biggest risk a person runs who tries to write as I do is the casual, superficial glance. "Oh, that's all there is to it," you know. I'm always quoting Mailer, who quoted Gide, who probably quoted somebody else – "Please do not understand me too quickly." That's one of the things I've always been frustrated by, so much so that sometimes I've been tempted to introduce deliberate obscurity – to make the reader read it more carefully.

METCALF: How would you justify yourself, then, for practising what is essentially an elitist art?

NOWLAN: I don't feel obliged to justify myself. If I were called to court like that poet in Russia and charged with wasting time I'd probably come up with some arguments in my own defence – but otherwise why should I bother? I don't think of myself as an elitist, but even if I did, and even if what I'm doing is absolutely useless – like Oscar Wilde saying, "all art is utterly useless" – even if that were so, I don't see where my elitism and useless would matter to anyone else. I have a friend who is a painter, Tom Forrestall, and one day I asked him what he'd been doing that afternoon, and he said, "looking at windfalls." He'd spent the whole afternoon simply sitting and watching the changing pattern of sunlight on apples. Now the president of the Canadian Chamber of Commerce would probably consider that a useless act. But who knows? Maybe there is a God like the god described in the Old Testament and he saw Tom Forrestall looking at the windfalls that day and decided that on second thought he wouldn't destroy the world. Maybe the whole show will fall apart if there ever comes a time when there's nobody left to look at the windfalls.

WORKS CITED

Alden Nowlan: Selected Poems. eds. Patrick Lane and Lorna Crozier. Toronto: Anansi, 1996.

Alden Nowlan: Selected Poems

A Review by Geoffrey Cook

Ten years after Robert Gibbs' *An Exchange of Gifts*, a new selection of Alden Nowlan's poems has been published in Canada. The volume edited by [Patrick] Lane and [Lorna] Crozier has, therefore, two purposes: to keep Nowlan's work in the public eye and to define his achievement. Whereas the latter will involve disputes, the former objective is significant because the past decade has provided a new audience. The new selection is a hundred pages shorter, and almost all the poems chosen by Lane and Crozier were included in Gibbs' edition. Since I am not a scholar, but an occasional reader of Nowlan's work, I won't debate the issue of a Nowlan canon. Rather, I'll comment on his poetry as representative of a new generation of Nowlan readers, since this is who the book will affect most. For it is meant to be a popular edition, thank god: there is a fine, brief introduction, a table of contents, no index or notes, and a reasonable 170 pages of poetry.

One of those who established a "Canadian voice" in poetry – the dominant form of which is the narrative of everyday life in free verse – Nowlan's work has remained vital. His lyrical "I" and quotidian experiences never bore us with egotism or banality because of his humility, humour, and compassion, his commitment to the detail and diversity of the world outside him and to the emotional one within, his radical fusion of the real and the imaginative, and the diversity and ingenuity of his forms — whether metrical and rhyming or rhetorical. Because that is his tact.

Much of Nowlan's work — his images, narratives, diction, rhythms, characters — is profoundly local. But the term "regionalism," which to many implies quaintness and thus irrelevance, hardly applies to such a careful and original art. See "A Mug's Game" (46). This condescending slotting of artistic achievement is the result of a sprawling country and self-absorption of centres of economic and political power. The definitive voices in Canadian culture can originate in places geographically removed from Toronto is something that we will just have to get used to, and our notion of culture should be correspondingly broadened. After all, in writing about Ypres — a sentimental nationalist's cry — Nowlan can, through imaginative recreation and attention to historical detail, disabuse himself of facile notions of nationality – "Yepres: 1915" (63). If he grew up with men "who never heard of Canada" – "Stoney Ridge Dance Hall" (31), his portrayal of these men and places makes Canada lucky to have heard of Alden Nowlan.

Concomitant with the portrait of Nowlan as a "regionalist" is that of him as a "plain speaker," a poet for those intimidated by "Poetry." That his work debunks the pretension of Poetry and Poetics is without question, but for all that's been said of his speaking plainly, Nowlan's vision is sophisticated and individual. His use of language and rhetorical or metrical form is also highly developed. In some of the poems of his late style, Nowlan's language achieves a transparency that is very rare. Poems like "An Exchange of Gifts" (68) – an intuitive, masterful Ars Poetica – or "He Sits Down on the Floor of a School for the Retarded" (151) – largely stripped of allusion, Biblical or poetic diction, symbol, metaphor, certainly metre and rhyme, and spoken in the careful voice of intimacy – work on us with such directness of speech and tone that any anxiety about "Poetry" evaporates. Our astonishment at the grace of these poems should not, however, blind us to the other virtues of Nowlan's poetry.

I say this because most introductions to his work imply that the late, "plain-speaking" free verse was an aesthetic and moral triumph over the early formal poetry. Good poems defy biographies; they disown their creators and endure the vagaries of fashion. "Canadian Love Song" (36) will remain an anthology piece, and it is, in part, the rigour of its rhymes and metre that makes it such an important poem. Formalism also lies behind the power of "Warren Pryor" (19), "Beginning" (12), and "All Down the Morning" (4). Nowlan's other devices include the deft use of dictions and allusions: from the Biblical, to the pop cultural, to the various discourses of the contemporary scene, and the vocabulary and rhythms of Maritime speech. He can manipulate imagery and symbol like a surrealist to effect horror – "Party at Bannon Brook" (25) – or passion – "The Wickedness of Peter Shannon" (51). His irony unmasks many conceits – "In the Operating Room" (52) – and is also used to deflate his own journalese, sentimentality, or pomposity at the most disarming moments. I don't mean to portray a calculating thinker, but to decry the naivety of sweeping statements that have been made about Nowlan's work. The celebrated "late style" was simply one of many; it is as rife as any early poem with artistry. The magical imagery and mysterious beauty of a poem like "A Song to Be Whispered" (154) couldn't have been achieved by any other poet working with traditional techniques. Joseph Brodsky wrote that rhyme and metre are tutors to the soul until the soul masters its art and dictates its own terms. That is, Nowlan's greatness of soul is also a result of wide-ranging dialogue with diverse techniques.

One of the most common themes in the work of Alden Nowlan is transformation. This theme includes: 1) the investment of the local with the mythic (through allusion) – "God Sour the Milk of the Knacking Wench" (10), "The Bull Moose" (28), "The Migrant Hand" (37), and "And He Wept Aloud, So The Egyptians Heard It" (40), "Written While Waiting for Another Chest X-Ray" (83); 2) the various studies in mistaken identity – "Looking for Nancy" (23), "Disguise" (27), "The Execution" (33), "Mistaken Identity" (72); and, 3) the intensity of an emotional experience (both imagined and/or recalled) – "I Icarus" (38), "At a Distance He

Observes an Unknown Girl Picking Flowers" (93),
"The Middle-Aged Man in the Supermarket"
(108), "You Can't Get There from Here" (155).
Alden Nowlan's genius was his ability to describe
the fluidity of the "real" and the "imaginary," decry-
ing the fallacy of their division and opposition. What
is real and what is imagined is a question of emotional experience, commitment and expression.
Nowlan creates the same emotional investment in
his readers: we trust him because of his honesty.

Which brings us to Nowlan's other most common theme: love. A collection of Alden Nowlan's
love poems would be, as Northrop Frye said of the
study of any genre, a liberal education in itself. But
then I've just looked through the table of contents
again and found that of the 123 poems in the selection, at least 100 deal with love! Nowlan shies from
nothing in his life-long analysis of love: bald, mov-
ing declarations and eroticism; furious lust and ter-
rible shames; graceful compassion and heroic
devotion; loneliness and longing; selfishness and bit-
terness; comic and tragic portraits of "deviation," the
politics of marriage and family . . . It would be foolish to summarize Nowlan's "position on love," the
point is how he can articulate the diversity of emotions "love" can be. The distinctive, embracing
authority of Nowlan's voice comes from his knowledge that the most vulnerable and suspect of emotional experiences is nevertheless the source of all
decency and dignity and hope. Reason enough to
write so often on a theme, though there is another.

Art has no closer sibling than love: they both demand vision and require acknowledgment of the real and the transcendent. There is no greater theme than love because love is the mortal equivalent of art.

We also must consider Nowlan's abounding humility. Nowlan won't let us forget that being human involves folly as well as pride. His confidence of tone − his intimacy − astonishes as much as the clarity and "accessibility" of his content. It is the bravery of this "confession" which distinguishes Nowlan's work. In the last poem of the collection, "The Fat Man's Poem" (172), the poet-character deconstructs his draft of a poem and its pretensions only to become entranced by the truthful lines he is writing. When he is finished "he reads what he has written / and he doesn't know whether to be proud or ashamed."

Grateful is what readers can be. *Selected Poems* proves Alden Nowlan's work has a richness and depth which always rewards. Academics exploring the themes and images, young poets learning how to speak their truths with the help of this great model, or lovers of poetry whose open ears enlarge their hearts, all owe thanks to Lane and Crozier for their edition: it keeps us reading a great soul.

WORK CITED

Nowlan, Alden. *An Exchange of Gifts: Poems New and Selected.* Edited and with an introduction by Robert Gibbs. Toronto: Irwin, 1985.

Various Persons Named Kevin O'Brien

Nowlan's Novel Response to the Critics

PAUL MILTON

The 1973 novel *Various Persons Named Kevin O'Brien* is something of an anomaly within the corpus of works attached to the name of Alden Nowlan. Nowlan is predominantly known as a writer of short poetry, short fiction and drama. The novel represents the only piece of extended fiction published under his name during his lifetime and with his assent. He had written an earlier novel, *The Wanton Troopers*, but had abandoned it after it had been rejected by a publisher; it was eventually published by Goose Lane Editions in 1988, five years after his death. *Various Persons Named Kevin O'Brien* also differs from Nowlan's more characteristic work because of its formal peculiarity. While Nowlan's poetry tends to be monologic in nature, working from the perspective of the lyric "I," the novel presents a dialogical text in which multiple narrative voices interact. The multiple narrative voices represent the protagonist, Kevin O'Brien, at various stages in his development: as a Nova Scotia child, as a rebellious adolescent, and as an adult who has moved away from home and now returns to view the home place with new eyes.

The novel also presents an interesting opportunity to see an author mobilize a variety of different discourses that impinge upon the creation of his artifact. By the time Nowlan comes to write this novel, he has already published several volumes of poetry and one volume of short fiction and has experienced the critical scrutiny of his work. The reception of Nowlan's early work often alludes to the question of his identity as a writer: is he a regionalist? If he is, then is that a good thing or a bad thing? If he is not a regionalist, then is he a "universal" writer? Indeed, the critics of his early work can, for the most part, be divided into specific camps based on their response to this question. There are those who see Nowlan's identification with the concerns and the particular identity of the Maritimes as a limiting factor, equating regionalism with parochialism. There are those who defend Nowlan's regionalism as an entirely valid approach to literary expression. Then there is a third group that justifies Nowlan's regional writings as being expressive of universal truths in a particular geographical and historical frame.

As Nowlan the author sees his reception determined by the interaction of these different positions, Kevin O'Brien sees himself in terms of the different interpellations that correspond to various phases of his life. His journey home permits him to juxtapose his various incarnations (regional child, rebellious adolescent, metropolitan journalist) and to listen to the polyphonic complexity of the voices that have attached to his proper name, the voices of the various persons named Kevin O'Brien. The journey home climaxes in the novel's final chapter in which Kevin confronts both his alienation from the home place and its expectations of him.

Mikhail Bakhtin's theories of the novel provide some context for understanding the position of *Various Persons Named Kevin O'Brien* within Nowlan's work as a whole. Bakhtin suggests that the novel is unique as a genre because of the way in which it integrates a variety of different stylistic unities into the novelistic whole, ranging from direct authorial narration through various forms of stylized oral and literary types of narration to the stylistically individualized speech of characters. For Bakhtin, "the novel can be defined as a diversity of social speech types (sometimes even diversity of languages) and a diversity of individual voices, artistically organized" (262). This matrix of different language uses permits a variety of dialogized social voices to operate within the text. The novelist welcomes and even intensifies this heteroglot quality in the text, constructing an authorial style which uses "words that are already populated with the social intentions of others and compels them to serve his own new intentions" (300). He goes on to suggest that this diversity is definitive of the novel:

> The orientation of the word amid the utterances and languages of others, and all the specific phenomena connected with this orientation, takes on *artistic* significance in novel style. Diversity of voices and heteroglossia enter the novel and organize themselves within it into a structured artistic system. This constitutes the distinguishing feature of the novel as a genre (300).

Within this context, Nowlan's turn to the novel affords him the opportunity to mobilize those various voices that surround his work, whether they be the critical voices that identify his work as problematically and narrowly regional or the voices of regional antecedents such as Ernest Buckler. These multiple voices enter the text through the consciousness of the protagonist Kevin who, as a child, demonstrates the influence of the regional voice, but as an adult, shows the influence of his job as a reporter at a metropolitan daily.

On his return home, Kevin experiences alienation because he has left the region and become an inhabitant of the city; as he has grown into his metropolitan adulthood, his childhood home has become subordinate in his mind. This alienation licences his self-representation as a detached observer who, as an author-figure and journalist, can objectively evaluate life in the region; as Kevin's stories show, he views his childhood home as ripe for criticism. Janice Kulyk Keefer points out that the narrative "successfully deploys two languages – that of the 'work beasts' of Lockhartville, and that of the educated middle class reader" (170). That middle class reader is analogous to the writers of the critical evaluations which condemn, apologize for, or defend the regional nature of Nowlan's early poetry.

In historicizing the reception of Nowlan's early work, it is important to note that Nowlan wrote from New Brunswick at a time when Canadian nationalism was gathering momentum and the national literature was becoming increasingly reified. His early works include *The Rose and the Puritan* (1958), *A Darkness in the Earth* (1959), *Under the Ice* (1960), *Wind in a Rocky Country* (1961) and *The Things Which Are* (1962). There is then a five-year hiatus, during which Nowlan battled cancer,[1] before the publication of the Governor-General's Award-winning *Bread, Wine and Salt* (1967) and the story collection *Miracle at Indian River* (1968). Although I hesitate to read too much particular significance into any literary award, I note that Nowlan collected the prestigious national award in 1968 for a book published in the year of the centennial of Canadian confederation, as nationalist a context as one might imagine in the Canadian mind. The irony here proceeds from the fact that his early poetry was seen by at least one reviewer as militating against the juggernaut of national identity.

Eli Mandel reviewed Nowlan's work three times in the early 1960s and discounts his regionalism, suggesting in one review of an anthology of New Brunswick poets that "the dreams which trouble the Maritimes are the same as those which disturb the long nights of Albertans and that nightmare is not *simply* a province named New Brunswick" (Rev. of *Five* 68). Later, addressing violence in *The Things Which Are*, Mandel says, "It's by the way to ask whether or not so much blood flows in New Brunswick; personally, I'm sure the province is no bloodier than Alberta" (Rev. of *Things* 280). He argues that regional voices threaten a long-awaited "single coherent shape" that Canadian poetry was approaching and instead:

> Contemporary poetry has mounted its horse and ridden off in all directions at once. There are still, of course, coterie poets: on the west coast, for example, a particularly limp group writing as though Vancouver's damp had somehow soaked their diction; on the east coast, a determinedly regional group muttering about farmers chopping off heads of chickens or wives, as the occasion demands (278).

Behind its colourful descriptions, this passage is motivated by the ideal of a literary identity that would erase regional difference in deference to a coherent national literature. In an earlier review of *Under the Ice*, Mandel questions Nowlan's credibility, saying "no one, surely, will mistake Nowlan's Faulknerian world of barn-burnings, bear-baiting, child-whipping, and Saturday-night dances for the actual Maritimes" (Rev. of *Under* 91). By invoking Faulkner, Mandel suggests that there is a trans-regional language of regional literature, that Nowlan and Faulkner achieve their sense of regionality by employing the same discourse.

Mandel was not the only critic to draw attention to regionalism as a detrimental feature of Nowlan's writing. Two other reviews of *Under the Ice* sound the same note. Miriam Waddington says that Nowlan "writes out of his isolated chip-on-the-shoulder Maritime culture" (71). Alec Lucas writes:

Regional poetry contains its own peculiar pitfalls, and Nowlan has dropped into some of them. His rhythms are often unduly irregular and his diction unduly flat. He seems to think that the poet best presents crudity by writing crudely. The result is not regional poetry but dogpatch verse (62).

Although Lucas does not condemn regionalism out of hand, he aligns Nowlan's regionalism with the backwoods caricatures of cartoonist Al Capp. The implication is clear: what Nowlan offers as literature is here received as cartoon.

Mandel, Waddington and Lucas write from the perspective of the Canadian academy. At the time of publication of these reviews, Mandel was a professor at the Collège Militaire Royal de St.-Jean in Alberta, Waddington was a social worker with North York Family Services (although she would join the English faculty at York University three years later), and Lucas was a professor at McGill University. Their reviews represent a national critical discourse operating from outside the region represented in Nowlan's work; critics from the Maritimes tend to view him differently.

Nowlan and the critics who defend him deny the existence of a New Brunswick school of writers; however, the response to Nowlan's work by Maritime critics suggests some degree of consensus about his importance in the region. Robert Cockburn, writing in *The Fiddlehead*, a Fredericton-based journal, attacks the critics who call Nowlan "a man of one theme" and claims that "there is more variety in *Under the Ice* and *The Things Which Are* than most critics seem to have been aware of" (Rev. of *Bread* 74). He drives the regional point home, identifying Nowlan as "of independent character and fortunate domicile . . . (and) largely free of the dictatorial antics of the covens of Montreal, Toronto and Vancouver" (76). If Mandel represents the extreme of one position, Cockburn articulates the extreme of the other pole. In the middle sit critics such as Peter Pacey who, in 1971, suggested that "there has been nothing regional, in a pejorative (*sic*) sense, in the poetry since the publication of *Bread, Wine and Salt*" (Rev. of *Bread*, 114). He adds that Nowlan uses the region as a metaphor for all humanity, implying the universal through the particular, using his own experience as the raw material of his art.

Similarly, while praising Nowlan's "acute feeling for place" (41), Keath Fraser distinguishes Nowlan's work from the Romantic detachment of an earlier major New Brunswick poet, Sir Charles G.D. Roberts, because the "consequence of calcified regionalism clutches Nowlan most noticeably" (42). Fraser's metaphor of "calcification" suggests a regionalism that has hardened and become lifeless. But in using the metaphor as a qualifying adjective, he allows the possibility of a life-affirming regionalism, a regionalism that has escaped calcification. Again, the critic's ideal becomes clear: "the regionalist at his best canalizes attention toward the aggregate experience of this individual, the Everyjoe who has served all masters in a *universal regionalism*" (44). Fraser's conclusion that Nowlan continues to grow as a poet even as his regional qualities endure suggests that regionalism serves the universalizing impulse.

In this critical discourse, then, regionalism becomes a charged word, possibly a slight, at very least an attribute that must be justified. The critical discourse assumes that a literature that attempts to represent its region faithfully simply demonstrates universal behaviour in particular surroundings rather than expressing a difference of view. As such, regional art is inferior to either national art or universal art and perhaps signifies an early stage in an artist's development. The process of development is the focus of Michael Brian Oliver's 1978 monograph *Poet's Progress: The Development of Alden Nowlan's Poetry*. Oliver establishes his position by invoking closure on the debate with the opening words of his first chapter:

> Alden Nowlan is no longer considered, by even the least perceptive critic, to be a "regional" writer. This recognition that his writing, especially his poetry, is not limited in its relevance to Atlantic Canada — or even to Canada for that matter — must be enormously satisfying to Mr. Nowlan personally, considering that the label "regionalist" has stuck to his reputation like a burr since the early ¬ 1960s when his career was just beginning. Today there is no longer any question: Alden Nowlan is an important poet, . . . Fortunately, nothing more needs to be said at this time about the fact of Nowlan's universal appeal (5).

Oliver goes on in this opening chapter to relate Nowlan's poetry to the nation-building thematic master-narratives of the 1960s and 1970s produced by D.G. Jones (*Butterfly on Rock*), Margaret Atwood (*Survival*) and Northrop Frye (*The Bush Garden*). So where earlier expressions of nationalist fervour dismiss Nowlan's poetry as narrowly local and parochial, Oliver seeks to recuperate it as a local manifestation of the national ethos within a homogenizing thematic context.

The criticism, taken as a whole, suggests that the trajectory of Nowlan's poetic development arcs away from the strongly local orientation of the earlier poetry to the work of the late 1960s, from which the regional "in a pejorative (*sic*) sense," to use Pacey's term, has been purged. Similarly, within the context of a study purporting to chart, in its suitably Bunyanesque title, the progress of a poetic pilgrim, Oliver characterizes Nowlan as having grown out of the region into the adulthood of the metropolis, dismissing the regional in favour of the national.

Little wonder then that the poet himself would want to reject any categorization of himself as regional. Nowlan responded to the "charge" that his poetry was "too regional" by saying that "most of the critics are people who want me to write about Toronto – which is smaller than the Maritimes" (Cockburn, "Interview" 10). In response to Mandel's assertion that no-one would mistake Nowlan's Maritimes for the actual Maritimes, Nowlan, who calls the review "a very kind and very good review," strikes a bemused tone: "Well, that is like saying my whole life has been a figment of my own imagination" (Cook 18). Elsewhere, he laments an apparent pedagogical need "to make believe that literature, like hockey, can be organized geographically (or otherwise) into leagues and teams" (Nowlan, "Something" 10).

Nowlan displays a degree of ambivalence to the critical discourse surrounding his early work. He expresses his frustration with the narrow critical view of his writing, and yet, in a 1963 interview with Gregory Cook, he speaks of his work in the same universalizing tone as that found in Oliver:

> I feel my work is less and less provincial because I myself am becoming less and less provincial. I mean a lot of my stuff has probably been provincial or parochial, but that isn't a failure in the material, it is a failure in me. I can write a lot better now than I wrote when I did the poems in *Under the Ice*. I'm ready to fight anyone who says that *The Things Which Are* is a book of regional verse. No, I'm not ready to fight them. Really, I care less and less about what people say about my poems and stories. No, that is false too, in a way, because I'm sensitive to praise and dispraise, but I don't let it affect my writing (19).

The hesitancy of his response here suggests that Nowlan struggles to find a way to articulate his frustration. At any rate, he is aware of the divided critical discourse surrounding his work. So when he comes to write *Various Persons Named Kevin O'Brien*, he can anticipate how it might be read.

Writing the novel, Nowlan, considered a conservative stylist in other genres, adopts a narrative structure that permits multiple voicing and an idiosyncratic sense of narrative time. The heteroglot narrative structure permits a debate between regional voices and non-regional authoritative voices across a number of character zones surrounding various persons named Kevin O'Brien.

Kevin appears in Nowlan's first attempt at the novel, *The Wanton Troopers*, a straightforward naturalistic narrative of Kevin's earlier years which focuses on the disintegration of his parents' troubled marriage. While there are similarities between the Kevin of the earlier novel and the Kevins of the later novel, there are significant differences that make it impossible to view the character as unproblematically consistent. The later novel enters into a dialogue with the earlier novel, recasting many of the same plot elements and characters in a very different and more lucid structure. The later novel includes those critical voices which Nowlan was only beginning to hear at the time he was composing *The Wanton Troopers*. In the earlier novel, Kevin views the region as wholly present to him; in the later, he re-enters his home town as an alien attempting to cope with the memories of absent people.

As the hometown boy who has travelled from home to make his name and is now returning, Kevin views himself at least partly as the embodiment of an objective critical discourse reflecting on a place that is now foreign to him. At the same time, the later novel marks Nowlan's return journey to his own earlier manuscript. As such, the theme of poetic development which emerges from the criticism intertwines with the theme of the protagonist's development both in *Various Persons Named Kevin O'Brien* and in the interstice between the two novels which feature Kevin as protagonist. *The Wanton Troopers* is the story of the child told by the novice author; *Various Persons Named Kevin O'Brien* is the adult story told by the mature author (Milton 61).

At the beginning of *Various Persons Named Kevin O'Brien*, Kevin stands at a particular point in his development. He is a mature independent adult who appears to have successfully escaped the repressive town of his youth. In his critical act of reading his manuscripts and in his professional role as a journalist, Kevin's consciousness becomes the conduit through which his own linguistic orientations at various points enter the novel. He is the privileged observer constructed by the various languages he speaks: the language of the region, the language of the metropolis, and, what constitutes the unifying thread, the language of mass media and pop culture. These three languages correspond roughly to the three positions within the critical discourse surrounding his work. As representative of the mainstream press and centralist ideology, Kevin is implicated in the subordination of the region. Language is the key here, and Kevin possesses that key; Keefer notes that language, which has liberated and alienated Kevin from the region, has been a factor in impoverishing "those who cannot aspire to correct or educated speech, and liberating those who can . . . This 'fictional memoir' is the story of a returned prodigy, not prodigal" (167). The prodigy, who has risen above Lockhartville, returns to examine it as it is, as he remembers it and as he has written about it. The result of this process can be examined through an analysis of the final chapter of the novel, "His Native Place."

Nowlan delivers the narrative through three sources in the text. The story of Kevin's return, which forms the frame narrative, is spoken by a third-person omniscient narrator. That third-person voice also relates Kevin's memories. A third source of stories is his manuscripts. The narrative alternates among the frame tale, the memories, and the memoirs, creating a rhythm that leads the reader to expect the novel will end with the omniscient narrator reasserting control. The book ends with a third-person narrative of Kevin's attendance at a dance on the final night of his visit. All narrative time frames coalesce in this story: it occurs in the present of the visit but is recollected some days later and, as such, is an event of the past.

To this point, Kevin's memory has not been called into question. Each of his memories has been admitted unchallenged by the narrator's voice, except for the ending of "The Hetherington Murder Case" which ends with an admitted lie (Nowlan, *Various* 117). In the final chapter, "His Native Place," the narrator foregrounds Kevin's lapses in

memory and a number of things that mediate
between Kevin and his ability to understand the
signs of his home village. In this chapter, Kevin
attends a dance with his boorish cousins, who goad
him into fighting with a man from a nearby village
over a local woman. The alienated Kevin has difficulty determining what is expected of him in this
fight in which, as a result of a lucky punch and a for-
tuitous fall, he beats the larger man.

Kevin is so removed from the village lifestyle
that, long before the fight, he is surprised to discover that "he had forgotten how, when his cousins or
any of the young men of Lockhartville greeted one
another, they invariably pretended they were about
to wrestle or box" (130). He blames his unfamiliar-
ity on faulty memory, which is ironic since Kevin's
memory has been the guarantor of authority for
much of the preceding narrative. Similarly, his memory of Estelle is discredited because he remembers
her as a child when she is now old enough to be an
object of sexual conquest. Again, when he hears the
familiar sounds of a local band, he doesn't recognize
the tunes they play. His memory fails him, and this
marks him as alien. Kevin's absence from Lockhartville, while it may have allowed him to grow in
metropolitan sophistication, has cost him in terms of
his familiarity with his native place. His knowledge
of his home town has become outdated. Throughout the novel, he has prided himself on his ability to
observe his home town with a perspective improved
by education and big-city experience; in this final

chapter, he is confronted by the fact that, in local terms, he is ill-educated and inexperienced.

If memory will not help him understand, he must seek another interpretive paradigm, mass culture. This provides a lexicon equally available to the villager and the city dweller, which facilitates communication although it does emphasize the differences: "television only serves to widen the gap between Lockhartville and the rest of the world, since little or nothing that appears on the screen has the remotest connection with what can be seen from the window" (3). At the same time, the city dweller claims a superior understanding of the images, as Kevin does in considering Estelle's miniskirt:

> It was funny, and a little pathetic, Kevin reflected, that nowadays girls in places like Lockhartville adopted exotic fashions more rapidly than most of their contemporaries in the cities, simply because their chief contact with the outside world was through television and their conception of what was fashionable was based on what was worn by Racquel (sic) Welch on the Johnny Carson Show (133).

Estelle's understanding is marked as naive or second-hand, and her attempts to be fashionable no more than mimicry. Kevin feels superior because he can distinguish between Estelle's ersatz fashion and authentic fashion.

But this structure is quickly reversed and the tables turned. Kevin notes that local country singer Tracy Devlin sounds like Eddy Arnold when he

sings "The Tennessee Waltz" and like Hank Snow
when he sings "I've Been Everywhere, Man." Again,
his superiority derives from his critical ability to see
the source through the mimicry. However, when
Tracy sings "The Waltz of the Wind," Kevin cannot
locate a voice that is being mimicked (134). Either
Kevin's knowledge of country music is, like his
knowledge of Estelle, behind the times, or he is
unable to recognize Tracy's own voice or the relatively unmediated voice of the region.

The climax of this concluding story comes in
Kevin's fight with Bob D'Entremont. His cousins
goad him into this local turf fight, which Kevin
would just as soon avoid. But to back down would
be to lose face. Still, he is uncertain how to approach
this fight and attempts to make sense of it in terms
of his understanding of movie fights. When his
cousins tell him that D'Entremont carries a knife,
again local knowledge fails him and he cannot be
certain whether they are teasing him or not. So he
turns to his knowledge of pop culture for assurance:
"In the real world men did not fight with knives.
Knife fights occurred only in films starring Robert
Mitchum and Lee Marvin" (137). When the fight
turns out to be a one-punch affair, he registers his
surprise by saying he "had always imagined these, his
people, battling like John Wayne and Victor
McLaglan in *The Quiet Man*" (142). Like Estelle's
conception of the outside world, Kevin's sense of
the region he has left behind depends upon patchy
memories supplemented by movies. His Maritimes

owe as much to Hollywood as to Halifax. For all his pretensions to superiority, Kevin's reliance on the universal discourse of popular culture keeps him in his place.

Kevin has aligned himself earlier with two models of the supposedly objective critical observer. By quoting Thomas Carlyle (5) and George Santayana (129), he has shown that he can function at least nominally in a learned academic discourse. But it is by virtue of his profession, journalism, that Kevin in most closely identified with an authoritative discourse. He thinks of headlines just before the fight while he still believes he might get out of it:

> If (D'Entremont) were sufficiently provoked he might come back next week with a half-dozen friends from his own village. But that was next week. And next week Kevin would be writing heads. "Government Agrees to Tariff Talks." Set in 42 Bodoni bold, centred on a three-column slug. "Middle East Crisis Worsens." Set in 48 Cheltenham bold for six columns reverse plate with arrow ends (139).

The headlines represent detachment, dealing with other conflicts far from Lockhartville and far from the headline writer. In his poetry, Nowlan has also parodied the notion of the detached journalist, notably in "The Execution" (33) where that detachment breaks down in a horrific way, and in "The Broadcaster's Poem" (106), where it remains unbreached only by circumstance. In the novel, the detachment disappears when the fight becomes unavoidable; the headline that comes to mind is

"'Man Stabbed to Death'... two columns, two decks, 48 Bodoni bold, with a 12-point, 22-em lead at top left of the local page" (140), all of which suggests an important story, at least in the most local of contexts.

The climactic punch destroys all Kevin's pretensions to detachment or alienation. He behaves exactly as the cousins expect. Significantly, as he leaves the dance with Estelle, Kevin is laughing. When Estelle asks him why, he utters the final words of the text: "'Damned if I know,' he answered" (143). The elevated tone has disappeared and he finishes with a swear word, "damned." The narrative does not return to its frame but implicitly refers farther back to the italicized preface, in which Kevin wonders whether he should "begin this book with a page containing nothing except a question mark" (1). The book ends with an answer of a sort: "Damned if I know." Earlier in the text, Kevin refers to some fictions as exorcisms (41), and it is perhaps the purgative force of the narrative that has removed the necessity to know.

His identity as a journalist depends upon his need to know on behalf of his readers, which leads to his reportorial investigations. That identity is suppressed at this stage of the story as he utters those final words sitting in the car with Estelle, away from the dance, amid fumes "like a naval smoke screen" (143), in a state where much interferes with perception, including the alcohol he has consumed. Then Kevin ends with a statement of the failure of knowledge; if the journey has been a quest for an understanding of himself and his regional roots, it has failed. Despite the cathartic climax of the punch, he has come to know nothing, only to experience pure viscerality. The verbal edifices that distance him from the region crumble at the moment of crisis and, as the narrative says, "he had never felt better" (143).

In naming Kevin's antagonist Bob D'Entremont, Nowlan alludes to another Maritime *Künstlerroman*, Ernest Buckler's *The Mountain and the Valley* which begins with the line "David Canaan had lived in Entremont all his thirty years" (Buckler 13). Like Nowlan's novel, Buckler's novel takes place in the Annapolis Valley. Both involve an artist-protagonist concerned with his ability to escape a home community from which he feels alienated because of his superior language abilities and his active imagination. The significant difference between the two situations is that Nowlan's protagonist is able to escape from his home while Buckler's fails to escape and dies in the trying. Buckler's novel exemplifies a tragic pastoralism in which the artist dies as a punishment for his sin of pride because he sees himself as superior to his neighbours. David Canaan is punished for failing to accept his home and for constructing the valley as a place from which he must escape.

In this context, Kevin's punch seems to respond in a comic fashion to some anxiety of influence harboured by his creator, Alden Nowlan; the stronger man, D'Entremont, stands in for the strong author-father Buckler who needs to be conquered in order that the younger writer might be freed. The plot of

The Mountain and the Valley presents a paradigm of the experience of the Maritime writer. In Buckler's version of the Maritime *Künstlerroman*, the artist who believes he must escape to realize his artistic vision dies. The artist who fails to recognize himself in the region dies unfulfilled. It is the oppressive, monologic quality of this paradigm with its narrative containment of the energies of the imaginative youth that Kevin takes aim at in this punch at D'Entremont. Ironically, however, this punch becomes the means by which Kevin recognizes himself as part of the world of the cousins who have goaded him into the fight. The blow that seems at one level to liberate him from the oppressive tragic vision of the regional artist even more surely demonstrates his connection to the world of Lockhartville.

The ending presents an ambiguity that suggests that Kevin dismisses any sense of development or progression beyond the region. The confident journalist who re-enters his childhood home does not progress to any greater knowledge or understanding. Indeed, the novel concludes with his colloquial profession of ignorance: "Damned if I know." As noted, taken in conjunction with the novel's opening allusion to a question mark, this statement suggests a circularity to the novel, a circularity that seems to reject the linearity of David Canaan's tragedy. It may also be a circularity that rejects the underlying pattern of the poet's progress, a pattern of development or growth from naive regionalist to mature nationalist.

Through the dialogical narrative structure of the novel, Nowlan displays for the reader both his awareness of the critical discourse that surrounds his work and its influence on him. Kevin O'Brien represents a refugee from his own home place who, in learning the language of the metropolis and adopting its perspective as his own mature view, learns a degree of disdain for the region from which he hails. The multiple Kevin looks upon himself as a fragmented creature who progresses from the parochial vision of his childhood to achieve the mature, nationalist view of his adulthood. But the final chapter of that novel acts to undermine Kevin's self-confident sense of having overcome the region. So Nowlan inscribes an ambiguous ending in the novel as Kevin's claims to have escaped founder on his re-absorption into the community and the dissipation of his sense of objective superiority. What remains is a regional statement that resists the paternalism of nationalist criticism and the tragic pastoralism of Ernest Buckler.

WORKS CITED

Bakhtin, Mikhail. *The Dialogic Imagination: Four Essays*. Ed. Michael Holquist. Trans. Caryl Emerson and Michael Holquist. Austin: University of Texas Press, 1981.

Buckler, Ernest. *The Mountain and the Valley* 1952. Toronto: McClelland and Stewart, 1970.

Cockburn, Robert. Rev. of *Bread, Wine and Salt*. *The Fiddlehead* 75 (1968): 74-76.

———. "An Interview with Alden Nowlan." *The Fiddlehead* 81 (1969): 5-13.

Cook, Gregory. "An Interview with Alden Nowlan." *Amethyst* 2.4 (1963): 16–25.

Fraser, Keath. "Notes on Alden Nowlan." *Canadian Literature* 45 (1970): 41–51.

Keefer, Janice Kulyk. *Under Eastern Eyes.* Toronto: University of Toronto Press, 1987.

Lucas, Alec. Rev. of *Under the Ice. The Fiddlehead* 51 (1962): 59–62.

Mandel, Eli. Rev. of *Five New Brunswick Poets. The Fiddlehead* 56 (1963): 65–68.

——. Rev. of *The Things Which Are. The Canadian Forum* March 1963: 278–80.

——. Rev. of *Under the Ice. The Canadian Forum* July 1961: 90–91.

Milton, Paul. "The Psalmist and the Sawmill: Alden Nowlan's Kevin O'Briens." *Children's Voices in Atlantic Literature and Culture: Essays on Childhood.* Ed. Hilary Thompson. Guelph: Canadian Children's Press, 1995, 60–67.

Nowlan, Alden. "Something to Write About." *Canadian Literature* 68–69: 7–12.

——. *Various Persons Named Kevin O'Brien.* Toronto: Clarke, Irwin, 1973.

——. *The Wanton Troopers.* Fredericton: Goose Lane Editions, 1988.

Oliver, Michael Brian. *Poet's Progress: The Development of Alden Nowlan's Poetry.* Fredericton: Fiddlehead Poetry Books, 1978.

Pacey, Peter. Rev. of *Between Tears and Laughter. The Fiddlehead* 93 (1972):114–16.

Waddington, Miriam. Rev. of *Under the Ice. Canadian Literature* 9 (1961): 70–72.

A Fully Human Poem

In Praise of Alden Nowlan

Thomas R. Smith

Alden Nowlan was born on January 25, 1933, in Hants County, Nova Scotia, a region so isolated that in the late 1950s Nowlan could say of it [in "Stoney Ridge Dance Hall"], "There are men here / who have never heard of Canada" (50). His poem "Summer" weds vivid images of the sense of loneliness and desperation Nowlan experienced as a child of the Depression in that windy, thin-soiled coastal valley:

> It's summer yet but still the cold
> coils through these fields at dusk, the gray Atlantic
> haunting the hollows and a black bitch barking
> between a rockpile and a broken fence
> out on a hill a mile from town where maybe
> a she-bear, groggy with blueberries, listens
> and the colt, lonesome, runs in crooked circles (33).

Freeman Nowlan, a tenacious and unimaginative man, managed to subsist by doing seasonal work in the sawmill and woods. Nowlan says of him [in "Growing Up in Katpesa Creek," an autobiographical essay], "My father worked for more than 50 years and never, to my knowledge, had a permanent year-round job in all that time, although God knows he was willing enough" (17). In "It's Good to Be

Here," Nowlan envisions his unpromising origins without apparent exaggeration:

> I'm in trouble, she said
> to him. That was the first
> time in history that anyone
> had ever spoken of me.
>
> It was 1932 when she
> was just fourteen years old
> and men like him
> worked all day for
> one stinking dollar (128).

The tactics and subterfuges imagination must resort to in order to stay alive in such a milieu is a theme Nowlan returns to obsessively in his poetry, fiction and essays. That no one of the accounts precisely jibes with any of the others serves to warn us not to take any of them too literally; yet all circle around a common truth.

Raised by his Irish grandmothers, Nowlan found an escape in literature, teaching himself to read at age five. By the time he reached adolescence he had read every book in the small regional library in Windsor. "I was Jack London reborn," [he told his son's high school principal, Ted Jones], "achingly aware of my enormous ignorance, gluttonously devouring any scrap of knowledge, reading great stacks of books on almost any imaginable subject" (12). At fourteen, Nowlan had read, in addition to the entire contents of the small regional library in Windsor, the Bible cover to cover three times, not so much from religiosity as the fact that it was the single book his father tolerated in their house.

Almost as soon as he was able to read, Nowlan began to write his poems and stories. What is most remarkable about these early literary efforts is that they were conducted in utmost secrecy, without evident support from family or community. In fact, Nowlan did not tell his father he wrote poetry until he left Windsor at the age of nineteen, to work as a reporter for the *Hartland Observer* in western New Brunswick. In rural Nova Scotia, as in so many other North American places of that time, literary interests were associated, if one happened to be male, with a shameful softness or effeminacy. "Even today," Nowlan acknowledged in a 1983 interview [with Lesley Choyce], "if I'm working on a poem and someone enters the room – anyone – I automatically cover the paper with my hands" (3).

In one of his poems of this period, "Weakness," Nowlan says: "My father hates weakness worse than hail" (30). Forcibly crushing such "weakness" invariably entailed throttling impulses for kindness, gentleness, and compassion toward other human beings. Nowlan's early poems reiterate a connection between cruelty and pride as acceptable public expressions; one may show kindness or affection only when safe from the threat of ridicule. In "Flossie at School" Nowlan secretively declares his liking for an awkward girl tormented by older boys: "And afterward I was ashamed / for crying when she cried" (31).

Nowlan's formal education ended after a month in the fifth grade, roughly matching the length of his father's. The oppressive environment of Hants County offered Nowlan little reason to hope that he would not follow Freeman Nowlan into a life of brute poverty and labor. Driven to seek solitude within himself, Nowlan was widely believed at this time to be mildly retarded, an added humiliation which surely deepened his empathy for the outsiders and misfits for whom he so passionately speaks in his poems and stories. One can imagine the agonizing frustration that led him to formulate [as he told Lesley Choyce], "The ultimate indignity is loneliness without privacy" (3).

Working in his teens as a pulp peeler, night watchman at a sawmill and road worker for the Nova Scotia Department of Highways, Nowlan managed at last to secure employment at the *Hartland Observer*, a province away, on the strength of a self-authored letter of reference. He writes of the chain of associations leading to his escape in "What Happened When He Went to the Store for Bread" with wonderful feeling for the small events which carry the awesome weight of contingency or fate:

> What would I have been if I hadn't left there
> when I did? I would have almost certainly
> gone mad; I think I might have killed somebody.
> But even if something else had saved me
> from madness, I would not be the same person.
> I'd have spent thirty years in a different world

and come to look at things in such a different way
that even my memories of childhood and youth
would be different; it might even seem to me now
that there was never anything to escape from (131).

Nowlan arrived in Hartland, New Brunswick in 1952, a move he says [in "Growing Up in Katpesa Creek"] that can't have been so very different from that of a raw Highlands youth coming down to the dour but safe Lowlands in the Scotland of, say, 1785" (24). He began to publish his poems in literary magazines in Canada and the U.S.A. In 1958 the University of New Brunswick published his first chapbook of poems, *The Rose and the Puritan*. Two large collections of poetry and an autobiographical novel soon followed. The early poems range over locales in Nova Scotia and New Brunswick geographically and culturally so consistent as to appear identical. One hears in these poems echoes of Edgar Lee Masters and Edwin Arlington Robinson, not only for the complete, self-referential world they create, but in the basic conception of character studies such as "Warren Pryor" and "Andy Shaw," which capture in a few sturdily constructed metric lines some deep tension between the intent and actions of their small town protagonists.

As marvelous and satisfying as this kind of poem is, by 1962 Nowlan had probably taken it as far as he wanted. Possibly its form had ideally suited a stage in his life he was now leaving behind. The early poems and novel linger over this Hants County past

in order to exorcise its ghosts and demons, an enter-
prise at least successful enough to allow him to
move on to new concerns and subject matter. A
reporter by profession, and an increasingly public
poet, Nowlan felt less pressure to remain hidden, to
artificially divide his public and private selves. Living under the tyrannous need for self-concealment,
one may see the conflicts of life in relatively simple
terms. But through his newspaper work, Nowlan
was now immersed in a world of far more complex
oppositions.

While the move to New Brunswick had freed
Nowlan from the poverty and repression of rural
Nova Scotia, the new life entailed its own hardships.
Low pay and long hours at the *Observer* dictated
Nowlan's holding down two or three jobs at once.
A novel, *The Wanton Troopers*, written on a Canada
Council grant in 1960 and not published until
1988, failed to rescue Nowlan from journalistic
drudgery. Nowlan took a full-time position at the
Telegraph-Journal in the more cosmopolitan Saint
John, where he lived with his wife Claudine and
their son John for the next five years. Successively
reporter, provincial editor and night news editor for
the *Telegraph-Journal*, Nowlan brings detailed first-
hand knowledge to his poems about politics and
current affairs. His sketch of Jamil Baroody, the
Saudi ambassador to the U.N., is keenly and dispas-
sionately drawn:

He tosses his pencil on the table

(not as a symbol of anything but simply because he is
    through with it)
and it bounces on the floor, out of reach, the first accident
to occur here tonight, and he glances down,
wondering where it fell, not because he cares
but because it is human
to glance down at things that have fallen (86).

Nowlan leads us beyond surfaces to the inner dignity of an old man in outworn service of "a king who
still lives in the fourteenth century," a king whom
Nowlan characterizes as "ignorant, cruel and bigot-
ed as the rest of us." We sense in such description
that Nowlan's interest in his subject extends far
beyond the more obvious contradictions of which
he has written incisively in the past – now he has
begun to value and praise the mysterious polypho-
ny that is the music inside each personality.

We notice also in this middle period of Nowlan
a sudden and dramatic expansion of the poet's emotional range and response, accompanied by an
enlargement of his stylistic repertoire. Now Nowlan
works frequently in a more naturalistic Williams-
influenced short line (occasionally in triads) and an
expansive long line owing much to Whitman by
way of Lawrence. This phase of Nowlan marks the
poet's mature engagement with history, both past
and contemporary, international as well as regional,
in courageous poems grappling in their half-
bemused, half-outraged way with demonology of
modern life [in "In Our Time"]:

The newspapers speak of torture
as though it were horseplay.
This morning a picture of a Congolese rebel
being kicked to death
was captioned *the shoe is on the other foot* (68).

In 1966 Nowlan was diagnosed with thyroid cancer
and underwent three major operations. This ordeal
is chronicled in such unsparing poems as "In the
Operating Room" and "Five Days in Hospital," in
which the poet wrestles [in the latter], Jacob-like,
with his own death:

I have discovered to my amazement
          that I am unable to believe
                    in my own death.
I know that I will die but I do not believe in it.
Then how is it there are times
when I am almost crazy with fear? (75)

These operations were successful and, although their
severity probably contributed to Nowlan's death by
weakening his system, he was to live another seven-
teenth years with no recurrence of the disease.
According to Claudine Nowlan [his wife], the crisis
had the positive effect of turning Nowlan's energy
away from journalism and toward serious literary
production.

As Robert Bly has emphasized in his introduction to Nowlan's first selected poems, *Playing the
Jesus Game* (New Press, 1970), fear is a persistent
theme throughout Nowlan's writing. If in the early
poems Nowlan's project is to confront and exorcise

fears of emotional and spiritual dismemberment in an environment hostile to the imagination and to art, in the poems of the 1960s Nowlan faces the internalized enemy who manifests physically in the form of disease or, projected outward, becomes a murderer of others. His poem about the assassination of Martin Luther King, Jr., "The Night Editor's Poem," drives its dagger straight into the part of us in unconscious collusion with impersonal forces that move against anyone attempting to liberate human beings (95). It is an honorable poem, one we in the United States could profit by knowing.

Nowlan's sixth poetry collection, *Bread, Wine and Salt,* won the 1967 Governor General's Gold Medal for Poetry, the highest honour for poetry in Canada. The poems are a product of the enormous creative energy released by Nowlan's encounter with mortality and subsequent rededication to his art. While the early poems, for all their bravery and precision, are mostly "about" other people (albeit with Nowlan hovering behind them), in *Bread, Wine and Salt* Nowlan reveals himself with disarming honesty and humor *as himself.* Nowlan knows he "contains multitudes," and his sense of the inner crowd and the difficulty of identifying a primary or "real" self among them reminds us at times of Neruda's playful orchestration of selves in *Extravagaria.*

In 1968 Alden Nowlan was appointed writer-in-residence at the University of New Brunswick in Fredericton, a post he was to occupy for the rest of his life. Freed from the economic necessity of having to divide his efforts between journalism and art (while choosing to maintain a regular column for the *Telegraph-Journal*), Nowlan produced five major books of poetry, from *The Mysterious Naked Man* (1969) to his late masterpiece *I Might Not Tell Every-body This* (1982). These were expansive years, both artistically and socially, in which Nowlan's stature and influence as a literary figure grew to fit his accomplishment, and in which he became recognized as a mentor to many younger writers in the Maritimes. He published a fine autobiographical novel, *Various Persons Named Kevin O'Brien*, short stories, drama, and essays, and the Nowlan household became a lively center for discussion of literature, politics and culture.

The poems appearing near the end of Nowlan's life are those of a man who has, in Lawrence's phrase, "come through." The atmosphere of struggle with dread, depression and terror has for the most part lifted; a spiritual combat has been fought, and largely won, in what Nowlan himself acknowledged as his "painful and only partial conquest of fear." A final fear has been recognized and confronted, one that Nowlan never names directly. The apparently light-hearted "In Praise of the Great Bull Walrus" offers a clue:

> I wouldn't like to be one
> of the walrus people
> for the rest of my life
> but I wish I could spend
> one sunny afternoon

lying on the rocks with them (113).

Nowlan was a physically large man, and here he uses the walruses to gently caricature himself. (He confessed in interviews a close identification with the bull moose in his popular early poem of that title; we are probably right in assuming that behind any large animal in Nowlan is likely to stand the author's stout figure.) The poem concludes:

> How good it is to share
> the earth with such creatures
> and how unthinkable it would have been
> to have missed all this
> by not being born:
> a happy thought, that,
> for not being born is
> the only tragedy
> that we can imagine
> but need never fear (113).

By his own account in "It's Good to Be Here" – "There's quinine, she said. / That's bullshit, he told her" (128), Nowlan came near not being born at all. As a boy shamefully aware of being a less than "wanted" child, Nowlan took an uneasy and self-punishing refuge in fantasies of annihilation. In his novels, Nowlan describes his often hilarious adolescent power fantasies, but we must look to the poems for his brooding on a self-cancelling more extreme than suicide, as in "Afterword to Genesis" where Isaac experiences, in addition to fear, "an inexplicable eagerness / waiting to be blotted out, swallowed up, made nothing" (88). The late poems enact Nowlan's decision to live despite the purely meta-physical and impossible yet inwardly oppressive threat of never-having-been.

Nowlan's final collection, *I Might Not Tell Everybody This*, is one of the best books published by a North American poet since mid-century. Its beauty and serenity are indicative of the author's having won through to a calm, human self-acceptance, a great achievement in an age defined by a fear of the self projected outward onto others and nature. In these poems we hear Nowlan's peculiar music at its clearest and most fluid, the base a unique and haunting play of irony and tenderness, each giving way to promptings of the other. The overarching effect is of an uninterrupted and spontaneous conversation between what Yeats called "self and soul," the self who knows the world and its betrayals and the soul who longs ceaselessly for its impossible desires. We see the triumph of soul and desire especially in the love poems and in the poems written for Nowlan's son. That triumph distinguishes *I Might Not Tell Everybody This* as a whole, and is the source of light that plays over even the darker areas in these poems. In "Bobby Sands," we glimpse Nowlan's Irish great-great-grandmother Mary Foley who died in County Wexford "with green stains on her lips, with her hands filled with grass," while English wagons hauled away the Irish grain:

            ... Being human, we

each of us can bear no more than a particle
of pain that is not our own; the rest is rhetoric.
Better to shed a tear for Mary Foley
than to rant or babble about suffering
that is beyond our capacity to comprehend.
And what of Bobby Sands? We talk too much,
all of us. In common decency, don't speak
of him unless you have gone at least a day
without food, and be sure you understand
that he loved being alive, the same as you (150).

The poem is both personal and rhetorical – Nowlan has learned to speak from both private and public centers at once, blending the two tonalities with unmatched confidence and grace. The dividing line between the personal and the political, a sticking point in recent discussions of poetry, has disappeared; that is to say, the poem has become fully human.

At the height of his powers as a poet, Alden Nowlan died unexpectedly of respiratory failure in Fredericton in June, 1983.

★

Alden Nowlan is widely considered to be the most important literary figure to appear in the Maritime provinces in the past thirty years. Clearly Nowlan manages, in writing truthfully and artfully of his specific place, to travel far beyond merely provincial concerns and speak to and for a greater audience. His 1970 selection, *Playing the Jesus Game*, brought Nowlan to the attention of U.S. audiences midpoint in his writing career, but has long been out of print. The time is right for a new American selection drawing on the complete range of Alden Nowlan's poetry. The present volume, limited to ninety-four of his best poems, will serve to whet readers' appetites for more of this unjustly neglected poet's work and add to the demand, already heard in Canada, for a comprehensive collected edition.

Providing a brief critical and biographical glance at Alden Nowlan's life and work, I've hardly mentioned Nowlan's stunning technical ability, which the reader might easily miss in assuming these poems, so wonderfully conversational and direct, spilled effortlessly from the pen. We know that Nowlan labored over dozens of drafts of a poem to achieve the illusion of naturalness. Lest anyone doubt Nowlan's mastery, let them look carefully at "Waiting for Her" (56) with its drumming, inwardly screaming crescendo in the second stanza and its controlled quiet – equally anxious – in the third.

Another of Nowlan's gifts to us is his care for truth. Having laboured most of his adult life in a profession now distrusted nearly as much as the politician's, Nowlan felt acutely the weight and expense of lies we live by, both the large public ones and the smaller private ones with which we comfort ourselves. He maintains a rigorous honesty, and in doing so communicates directly with some truth-organ in us that knows when it is or isn't being lied to. This discipline affords Nowlan a sophistication that places him light years ahead of many North

American poets who persist in simple-minded antagonisms, assigning all evil to others. Reading Nowlan, one feels honored, as when reading Whitman, by the sheer human capacity for both good and evil (and the ability to choose between them) the poet has assumed for himself and his audience.

One measure of an artist's mastery is the extent to which we are made to care about his or her story. Alden Nowlan makes us care intensely about his story. Specific in its particulars, Nowlan's story partakes of some general struggle of the modern soul to surmount shame, poverty, powerlessness, and fear to enter the full richness of a human life. In this, Nowlan bears a striking resemblance to James Wright, who escaped the meanness of life in an Ohio factory town and in spite of personal hardship achieved the luminous gift of his poems. Both Nowlan and Wright identified profoundly with society's outcasts. Like Wright, Nowlan was constantly aware not only of the violence around him but of his own capacity for violence. The key, Nowlan suggests in poem after poem, is knowledge of self, as in "Confession," where, reflecting on the lust of a murderer-rapist, Nowlan tells his lover,

> [I] might love you less
> if I did not know
> that other one so well
> had not talked with him
> far into the night (79).

Visiting the Maritimes in 1989, six years after

Nowlan's death, it became clear to me that many Canadians hold a Nowlan poem, such as "He Sits Down on the Floor of a School for the Retarded" (151) or "Weakness" (30), in a place of esteem similar to that reserved in the United States for a Wright poem [in *Above the River* such as "A Blessing" (143) or "Lying in a Hammock at William Duffy's Farm in Pine Island, Minnesota" (122).

[In his edition of Nowlan's first posthumous selected poems, *An Exchange of Gifts*] the Canadian poet [and literary executer of the Estate of Alden Nowlan] Robert Gibbs has described Nowlan's process – which applies not only to individual poems but to the general shape Nowlan's life and work took unfolding – as "a working through from self-esteem and self-doubt to an awareness of vanity and limitation in himself and others, and beyond that to a wider awareness lodged in compassion" (xiv). As difficult as Nowlan's circumstances undoubtedly were, alleviating his own suffering seems never to have been the final goal of his struggle as an artist or as a man. What is most beautiful in his poems, I think, is Nowlan's refusal, grounded in a sure knowledge of human moral limitations, to accept isolation and alienation, a refusal which leads him toward progressively deeper acts of compassion and generosity.

That isolation Nowlan fought to overcome has its natural breeding ground in small towns all over North America. I was a boy during the 1950s in a paper mill town in northern Wisconsin, in its way as hopeless and brutal as those Nowlan describes. In such places, one feels beneath the sun-lit surface of a cheerfully maintained normalcy a tremendous undertow of darkness: the bad luck, cruelty, disease, morbidity, and madness which rush into the vacuum created in the human community when a tradition-al culture rooted in place is left behind. Many in our time respond to this sense of threat by retreating into numbness, alcoholism, television, and "queer religions." Nowlan knows how difficult it is to maintain under such circumstances the alertness and openness that the practice of art requires.

That a mostly self-educated man without visible support in his early years should decisively over-come fear, confusion, and rage to produce, in nine full-length collections, one of the most deeply hon-est and humane bodies of poetry on our continent in this century is astonishing. In an era in which much North American poetry is dimmed by passiv-ity, lack of desire, and a readiness to mock the hard-won achievements of past civilization, Alden Nowlan's poems demonstrate what is still possible when one has courage to face without denial the worst truths of our time and ourselves, and desire to honour the still deeper truths of the heart.

[An introduction to *What Happened When He Went to the Store for Bread* (1993)]

WORKS CITED

Nowlan, Alden. *What Happened When He Went to the Store of Bread*. Edited and introduced by Thomas R. Smith; a fore-word by Robert Bly. Minneapolis: Nineties Press: St. Paul:

Distributed by Ally Press Centre, 1993; an afterword by Thomas R. Smith, in the second edition. Thousands Press, 2000.

Alden Nowlan, "Growing Up in Katpesa Creek," in *Double Exposure*, p.17, Brunswick Press, Fredericton, NB, 1978.

Ted Jones, "Alden Nowlan: Required Reading," p. 12, *New Brunswick*, Vol. 8, No. 3-4, New Brunswick Information Service, Fredericton, NB, 1983.

Lesley Choyce, "Interview," p. 3, *Pottersfield Portfolio*, Vol. 5, Porters Lake, NS, 1983-84.

Nowlan, Alden. *Playing the Jesus Game.* Trumansburg, N.Y.: New Press, 1970.

Wright, James. Above the River: The Complete Poems, Farrar, Straus and Giroux and University Press of New England, 1990.

Robert Gibbs, "Introduction," p. xiv, in Alden Nowlan, *An Exchange of Gifts: Poems New and Selected*, Irwin Publishing, Toronto, 1985

"My Family Was Poor"

Thinking About Alden Nowlan and Class

THOMAS R. SMITH

Canadian readers sometimes ask what drew me, as an American poet, to Alden Nowlan's work. Most of my reasons I've outlined in the introduction to this book. In North American literature, Nowlan is a curiously amphibious creature, having as much to say to Americans about their history as to Canadians about theirs. While it's generally true that Canadians know far more about the politics and culture of the U.S. than vice versa, I recognized in Nowlan an extraordinary grasp of affairs "south of the border" that illuminated not only the outward history of my own nation, but, so to speak, its inner, hidden, psychological and spiritual history. In particular, there are poems specifically grounded in American events which I was convinced U.S. readers could profit from knowing, such as "The Night Editor's Poem" (95) about the murder of Dr. Martin Luther King, Jr.

Since writing the 1993 introduction, I've realized that one of the things speaking to me most forcefully in Nowlan's work has been his enormous bravery and truthfulness in confronting the reality of class, a subject that most American poets – especially today, when many succumb to the trend to reinstate poetry to its mid-century status as an accoutrement of the privileged life – studiously avoid. In this afterword I would like to address more fully Alden Nowlan's awareness of class and his refusal to ignore the poor.

Class is a word that contemporary Americans often ignore, apparently believing it is not relevant to our society. We do so against our own best interests, in the same way that many working class people voted for Ronald Reagan in 1980 and 1984. Didn't the American Revolution overturn the class system once and for all? "We have no royalty, we are a democracy," insist the publishers of *People Magazine*, network TV producers, and the CEOs of the multinational corporations, whom no one in the media seriously challenges. Meanwhile, inequities continue to flourish in the shadow of our denial of class. Wendell Berry has provocatively argued in *The Hidden Wound* that the evil we call racism is also, frequently, an unexamined class bias: A prejudice against Black manual laborers masks a class prejudice against all manual laborers, for instance.

I am continually in awe of the clean, honest and alert way Nowlan confronts and assumes the reality of class in poems such as "Britain Street" (65), "Warren Pryor" (41) and many others, without left-wing hand-wringing and without right-wing blaming of the poor for their poverty. In fact, Nowlan provides a model of remarkably compassionate though unsentimental clarity in his willingness to speak truthfully for and about the poor. As he says, "there's no point in poetry / if you withhold the truth / once you've come by it" (63). He knows that portraying what is admirable about the underclass without portraying their flaws is worse than a lie – it is a more insidious form of condescension. In this recognition, he has few peers, especially among recent poets (Wesley McNair in Maine is an exception, as are the novelists David Adams Richards and Carolyn Chute in Canada and the United States, respectively).

In "What Colour Is Manitoba?" Nowlan jumps fearlessly into his personal experience of class, undeterred by the shame that usually inhibits our attempts to speak of it:

> My family was poor.
> Not disadvantaged curse
> that word of the sniffling
> middle classes, suggesting
> as it does that there's
> nothing worse than
> not being like them.

This idea "that there's / nothing worse than / not being like them" is the secret engine driving the advertising industry; in reinforcing consumer insecurity, advertising contributes to a cultural uniformity in which the poor are viewed, increasingly, as being *economically incorrect*. In a "new world order" in which economics, and not religion or morality, has the final say, being poor implies some fundamental wrongness of being:

> It's as if a chemist
> had analyzed a river

and declared that its water
was an inferior form of fire (122).

In his empathy with clerks, soldiers, pulp cutters, prisoners, and illiterate people Nowlan escapes the class prejudice by which many liberal, college-educated whites claim tacit superiority over persons who do the actual physical work of maintaining society.

In all periods of his writing, from the early story-telling poems set in rural Nova Scotia and New Brunswick, through his last in which he courageously and often humorously grapples with his own psychological complexities, Nowlan is keenly aware of an inherent cruelty in human relationships, a great many of which are informed differences. He recognizes the cruelty in regional prejudices, as perpetrated by the CBC commentator who reports patronizingly of the poet's visit to Toronto [in "A Mug's Game"]:

> ...The purpose of such readings is to give writers
> from unlikely places like Hartland, New Brunswick,
> the chance to communicate
> with others
> of their own kind (70).

I should make clear that I don't believe Nowlan consciously approached the act of composing poems with the sense of agenda my examples might suggest. Rather, he seems to have habitually written from an emotional immediacy that permitted direct access to all of the great themes present in his life, which included his cumulative experience and observation of class injustice. On a level more fundamental than that of class awareness, Nowlan's moral universe consists of the countless acts, both small and large, of cruelty and kindness which make up human life. Class prejudice falls firmly within the category of that public cruelty present in Nowlan's upbringing, which he identified early, and honorably anatomized and deplored throughout his career.

However, Nowlan cannot comfortably be drafted into the ranks of such consciously proletarian poets as Milton Acorn and Thomas McGrath. Staunch Marxists both, they rose from similarly impoverished roots to become "people's" poets. As a rule, Nowlan leaves the politics to us; his job is to portray human beings of all kinds – including the poor – in all their frightening complexity, humanity, and similarity.

It is easier to distance ourselves from the poor if we consider them an inferior species, "an inferior form of fire," rather than persons like ourselves, conceived in the full potential of a human life and whose nature has been acted upon by mysterious forces, only some of which are sociopolitical. In his novel *For Those Who Hunt the Wounded Down*, David Adams Richards remarks of his protagonist Jerry Bines that "nothing [he] did or said, or how he acted, could make any difference, in ways that are real" (116). This is a heartbreaking sentence, one that Nowlan would have understood perfectly. An unspoken societal agreement that the poor can do nothing that will make a difference "in ways that are real" breeds an impotence that, perhaps even more than stark economic desperation, drives individuals to acts of "senseless" violence. Given such a premise, naturally a CBC commentator's utterance will count for more than any "provincial" poet's! Seen from this perspective, Nowlan's poems are an attempt to redeem the struggles of people of low station and limited resources to make "real" differences.

On a psychological level, Nowlan understands that there is a poor person – or even several – inside each of us, adding a necessary dimension to Christ's statement, "The poor you always have with you." If this weren't so, if poverty did not somehow exist at every person's core, no matter their degree of outward affluence, we would probably find the literal poor far less threatening.

Despite a compassion for the poor bred in the bone, Nowlan seems never to have fallen into the trap of debilitating class resentment. One might say his imagination never went the politically correct route of symbolic regicide. A Canadian poet who was a friend of the Nowlans once showed me a charming piece of memorabilia, an invitation to a party at their house in Fredericton celebrating the marriage of Prince Charles and Princess Diana. I remember my puzzlement at this Canadian fascination, this contradictory reverence for royalty on the part of a poet who has spoken as well as anyone in this century for the downtrodden. More recently I recognize as a sign of health that Nowlan's sympathy with the poor did not obliterate what psychology might call his "grandiosity," which allowed him from boyhood to fantasize himself conqueror, Emperor, or even God. Although Nowlan all his life sustained the wounding of early poverty, his inner sense of grandeur was apparently not one of the casualties. Had Nowlan lost his capacity for vicarious participation in nobility, it's doubtful he'd have maintained, in conditions overwhelmingly hostile to self-esteem, the gentle arrogance necessary for becoming an artist.

Psychologically, Nowlan's triumph over the meanness of his origins lay partly in his ability to accept both the high-born and low-born persons in himself, the king and the outlaw, the wielder of power and the victim of power, a tolerance which, in turn, bred tolerance for others. His artistic achievement was to create an *oeuvre* broad, deep, and diverse enough to include the whole community of his clamouring selves.

I sense that this radical inclusiveness runs against the grain of current literary tastes in the U.S. (and unfortunately in Canada, too), which seem to tend now toward the upscale and the superficial. The poet Alice Van Wart brought *What Happened When He Went to the Store for Bread* to national visibility in Canada in an essay in *The Globe and Mail*, but no publication of similar standing in the U.S. has recognized this book to date. One would be naive, in the present climate of affectless, theory-dominated writing promoted by postmodern English departments, to expect academic critics to look up from their Jorie Grahams and John Ashberys long enough to notice a plain-spoken Maritimer who eschews abstraction and aims for the heart.

Yet Nowlan now enjoys, at the very least, a vigorous underground reputation in the U.S. Readers who value emotional candor and generosity of spirit buy multiple copies of *What Happened When He Went to the Store for Bread* to give as intimate gifts; therapists read the poems at professional conferences; ministers incorporate them in their sermons; people not identified with literary movements or circles embrace Nowlan as a long-lost brother. Occasionally I hear from or about them. Nowlan's poetry continues to find passionate advocates among poets and poetry lovers weary of the aridity and self-centeredness that make so much current poetry thin, unrewarding fare. When readers tire, as they inevitably must, of our period's gentrification and numbness, Alden Nowlan's fully human poems will still be there for them. In this respect, it may be that Nowlan's time has yet to arrive.

[Afterword: *What Happened When He Went to the Store for Bread* (2000). An earlier version of this essay appeared in a special Alden Nowlan issue of the Canadian literary magazine *The Pottersfield Portfolio* in Halifax, NS, for Fall 1997.]

WORKS CITED

Nowlan, Alden. *What Happened When He Went to the Store of Bread*. Edited and introduced by Thomas R. Smith; a foreword by Robert Bly. Minneapolis: Nineties Press: St. Paul: Distributed by Ally Press Centre, 1993; an afterword by Thomas R. Smith, in the second edition. Thousands Press, 2000.

Wendell Berry, *The Hidden Wound,* Toronto: HarperCollins Canada, 1989.

Richards, David Adams. *For Those Who Hunt the Wounded Down*. Toronto: McClelland & Stewart, 1993.

I Went to Meet Alden Nowlan

David Adams Richards

I went down to Fredericton to meet Alden Nowlan, the man from Desolation Creek, N.S., a found-
ing member of the Flat Earth Society, whose charter
relinquishes Earth to the abyss somewhere off the
coast of Newfoundland; member of the inner court
of King James Stewart, the Stewart monarchy in
exile (yes, Stewart – the French changed the spelling
to Stuart); honorary doctor of laws, like one of his
heroes, Sam Johnson – both prodigious towering
men, with grave knowledge and a curious softheart-
edness, a more curious vulnerability to be a target of
their times; like Sam as well, a brilliant conversation-
alist – more precisely, what is a Maritimer trait, a
"monologist"; a cook, and a good one; a secret
watcher of daytime soaps, an intentional lover of bad
movies – which is, to my way of thinking always a
sign of greatness, a self-taught reader by four years of
age, with, by the age of thirty-five, a library containing thousands of volumes of works on every possible subject, and thousands of his own poems; a
reader of five newspapers a day, who quit school in
Grade 5 to work in the woods, which made him the
only poet in the country deemed functionally illiterate by Statistics Canada – a fact he was whimsical-
ly proud of; a large, imposing, generous,
self-deprecating, hard-drinking, chain-smoking,

complex, irascible, irritating wonder of a man who hand been born in poverty, the son of a woodsman and a teenage girl, in the Depression year of 1933 in rural Nova Scotia.

I went down to meet Alden Nowlan, which might have been a title to one of his own poems, and I could quote dozens of them.

I would quote his poems and watch in Sydney, Australia, or Brisbane, or Virginia, or New Orleans, or London, peoples' faces light up for the first time at the man's genius – recognize themselves in him, and hear in his simple, straightforward words some great eternal wisdom. It was a wisdom tinged with sorrow, that always came, it seemed, in the form of a parting between friends said at the door on a cold winter evening.

The last time I quoted them (I leave it to others now), people asked about him, at the writer's conference in Brisbane, Australia, in 1993:

"Where is he from?"

"Where can I get his poems?"

"What are the names of his books?"

"Did he win the Nobel Prize?"

One middle-aged woman whispering in my ear: "His *Cousins* – you know a secret – I grew up like that, here in Australia, that's what I've been trying to say in my work, but I never heard anyone say it like that. Can I write to him? Is he Canadian?"

"He would love you to – and he would answer – but he is gone from us," was the only answer I could give.

★

He lived at best a precarious childhood, growing up in the Mosherville-Stanley area of central Nova Scotia. There are scenes in the novel about his childhood, *The Wanton Troopers*, that are truly horrific. But as he once said, children can exist in a world adults would go mad in.

By the time Alden was 33, he would have the first of his major operations for throat cancer – the doctor telling him that the chances of his living through it were about the same as a Canadian soldier living through the landing at Dieppe in 1942. When the doctor told him he had cancer, he burst out laughing. It seemed so strange. He had gone to see about a sore throat.

He lived through the first operation, and a second one, and a third – losing the muscles in his shoulder as a result – and as a result of that growing a lion-like beard to hide the scars on his throat that his closer friends would sometimes see whenever he sat in his den in his housecoat and leather slippers. He did not quit smoking.

Still, why would he not live through those operations? He had lived through so much before this. Abused as a child of poverty – tormented, abandoned, beaten. Thought of as retarded, and mocked by men and boys he knew, spending years in isolation – discovering mocking came because of their fear of him. He learned over time how prevalent this would be.

Finally he left home at nineteen, never to return, to take a job at the newspaper in Hartland, N.B., *The Hartland Observer*, lying about certain qualifications he never had and, as it turned out, never needed. There he formed friendships with people such as [former Premier and future Senator] Hugh John Flemming and young Richard Hatfield [subsequently Premier], the latter a friend he would not desert. In fact, Nowlan would desert so few in his life. Even his father, who treated him cruelest of all, he did not desert. His poems about and his letters to his father reflect this. In his 1974 novel, *Various Persons Named Kevin O'Brien*, he admitted that he was the only person in the world who ever feared his father, one line that says more than any report on the subject ever could.

His life as a child, he once said, was the life of Huckleberry Finn – not the romantic freckle-faced kid – that, he said, was Tom Sawyer. No the world of Huck Finn was both violent and terrifying, and Twain made sure he let us know it was. So, too, did he.

★

I was on my way to see Alden Nowlan, on my motorcycle on a summer's night, shifting down through the turns on the Killarney Road in Fredericton, during one of the last summers of his life – I did not know this then, of course, though I now suspect he must have. Looking back, he was probably forty-eight years old, so he had done some living. And more than his share of suffering, though he almost never complained and, like James Joyce, had a resolute will to forge out of the smithy of his soul his own destiny. There is something great in that attribute, that rare ability to be one's own man, and to (as Chekhov said) "squeeze the slave from my soul."

Destiny it was. And it was his great intellect, matched with a brave heart, that saw him through. He was a friend of Hatfield and Dalton Camp [journalist and Progressive Conservative brain trust], of Irving Layton, knew Ernest Buckler, and Pat Lane, and John Newlove; conversed with Morley Callaghan and corresponded with Henry Miller; a friend also of Stompin' Tom Conners; a friend of ordinary men and women everywhere. Sometimes he would pick and area code out of the telephone book late at night and phone the operator in a small town in Virginia or New Mexico to have a chat. Knowing loneliness and human nature, he knew they were often happy to have a person listen to them for a change.

He said he would make a great old man – but he said it the way people do who test the waters, hoping God is listening. At times he matched his age against those whose work he respected, and felt some achievement in outliving them, because death was always an intimate presence.

He had outlived Keats (and once he smiled and said to me, "Well, except for Thomas Chatterton, who hasn't?). He had outlived Emily Bronte, Shelly and Byron, and D. H. Lawrence, Dylan Thomas, Brendan Behan and Malcolm Lowry. He was the last to think that earthly longevity was the measure of any man or woman (just look at the names mentioned), but it was no less true that to keep going and keep writing would be fine with him.

Of them all, Keats was his favourite. Not the Keats of schoolbook misinformation, the wispy English Romantic, but the tough life-loving, 5-foot-4 boxer and walker, glorious champion of the underdog, named "Junkets" by Leigh Hunt, writer of brilliant sonnets and odes who died forsaken by the public an age before. "The magnificent Red-haired Runt," Alden Nowlan called him. Nowlan shared more in common with him than he himself might have thought. Both early on were such bleak prospects and suffered illness, in silence, to almost the same degree.

There is a picture of Nowlan taken when he is about thirteen – a runny nose, a malbuttoned checkered woolen bush jacket, a desolate landscape behind him, a lonely gaze out at the camera toward some faraway place. A haunted sadness encompasses everything.

From this picture it would seem amazing to some that he wrote at all – that he wrote poems, astonishing. But that he wrote many of the finest poems ever written by anyone in Canada – a country that in very many ways ignored him – miraculous.

His first poems were traditional, but infused with great power and perception. Think of that ill-fed skinny kid looking at the camera, with scared and haunted eyes, his jacket missing buttons and his clothes tattered, and then read these poems conceived in that childhood of beatings and tattered clothes, and written in youth.

★

He went to the Saint John *Telegraph-Journal* in 1963 on the strength of his editorial ability, to Fredericton in 1968 on the strength of his poetic genius, as writer in residence at the University of New Brunswick, after he won the Governor General's Award for a collection called *Bread, Wine and Salt*.

In Fredericton came his golden age, or golden moment – the flourishing of his genius, of his temperament, the legend surrounding both his enormous talent and his drinking. His poetry continued to change, to become more analytical, observant and objective, a strong narrative voice emerged, psychologically penetrating, always sympathetic to its subject. He was trying in a way for pure poetry – which meant pure truth. As always, humanity is everywhere in his work – in his world you cannot exist without it.

At his house on Windsor Street in Fredericton, called of course, Windsor Castle, Nowlan entertained, met other writers and poets, started his pet projects and societies (the world was so utterly self-absorbed as round, why shouldn't we claim it flat); it seemed to still have purpose then. So many of his friends were descendents of Irish and Scottish clans who had fought the British at every turn – why not reclaim the throne, even if in exile in New Brunswick?

He was interviewed about these claims by rather literal people who did not catch on to the serious-ness of it all, or the joke. And Nowlan was a master of the understated in both.

Like the seriousness accompanying the joke played on the world when he was given the task as a young man, of measuring the Hartland Bridge, to reassert its claim as the longest covered bridge in existence. Nowlan measured it from one side to the other and then, for good measure, he continued across the street, proceeding until he came to a stop at his desk in the Hartland *Observer* office. Walking backward all the way, he finished his measuring when he was able to sit down.

And though he helped reassert the right to the throne for the descendents of Bonnie Prince Char-lie, he was, in the end no British hater – that was a small man's part. Besides, he cared too much about British literature and tradition.

Meeting Prince Charles in the 1970s, he com-mented that he like his beard.

"But my mom disapproves," the Prince said.

"Ah, Sir, what mom doesn't?" Alden Nowlan offered.

When meeting June Carter Cash, he said: "Miss

Carter I have long been of the opinion that you
have the sexiest right knee in all of show business."

"Thank you very much for noticing," Carter
Cash said, and lifted her dress to show him the knee.

*

His parties where filled with people from disparate
walks of life, who had totally different opinions and
political stripes, who might not speak to each other
anywhere else. At Alden Nowlan's they found safety.
The premier could be there, and so too members of
the Opposition, a single mother on welfare sitting
beside a corporate lawyer, sound poets adrift in the
world, and young men with their daddies' money,
rural-bred soldiers from Gagetown sitting beside
urban pacifists, wearing peace beads, sharing ciga-
rettes from the same pack. As Gorky said of Tolstoy,
so someone might have said of Nowlan: "As long as
this man lives no one will be an orphan."

Of course, he could not live. That is always the
secret.

Someone once told me that Alden Nowlan only
attracted youngsters, and that people his age were
wary of him. Although he had a great many older
friends, that is still true in part, but it was not Nowlan's fault. The young sought him out, as the young
must have sought out Emerson, or Socrates. Why? It
is simple. The young have to.

He was comfortable with the young. They came
to him because he for many years he was the first

adult they ever heard speak like an adult should speak. Many were would-be poets, and he was a mentor. Some his own age, especially from the university, were wary of him because, just like Beethoven with the nobility, he could not bow easily to those who had not come to knowledge within the harsh life-and-death parameters he himself had faced.

But the young came. He never so much instructed them, but listened to them. Perhaps, who knows, they were taken seriously for the very first time in their lives. It is literally true that there was a time his house was filled with people young enough to be his sons or daughters.

★

I went down to meet Alden Nowlan, but the lights were out, and I did not want to wake him at the door. I turned my motorcycle around in the summer air, and shifted through the avenues of people already asleep.

He did not know of this impromptu visit, and the next time I visited was one of my very last.

He was watching Peter Ustinov's documentary on Russia: " Lo Davy," he said, and got up to turn the television off.

"No, Alden," I said, not wanting to disturb his program. "Please leave it on."

"Nonsense," he said, "If Peter Ustinov in on TV and David Adams Richards enters the room − off goes the television." And he made that great jerking motion with his arms.

I sat down. He was silent a long moment. The he looked over at me and, with a kind of cherub-like smile, shyly added: "Mind you, Davy, if David Adams Richards was on television and Peter Ustinov walked in – well then, what I mean to say is, well, you know – the TV just might go off, too."

At the last of his life he was left alone, as old friends departed for other places, and lives changed. The great court was over and often he sat in his den in solitude.

Some made excuses, saying he was difficult and his best days were over. Noble of them … to be entertained by him on his best days. And he – well, he was still writing great poems, about the martyr-dom of Bobby Sands, about going to a "school for the retarded" to speak to children, or summing up Boswell's 2000,000-word biography of his old friend Sam Johnson.

*

I have often wondered what Canada gave Alden Nowlan. I have never come up with a satisfactory answer.

I his great poem *Ypres: 1915*, he asked, in a curi-ous way, if he even had a country – and more sub-tly, though never spoken, if Canada of today deserved the bravery of those kids fighting along the line, the first time the Germans used gas:

Perhaps they were too scared to run.
Perhaps they didn't know any better
— that is possible, they were so innocent,
those farmboys and mechanics, you only have to look
at old pictures and see how they smiled.
Perhaps they were too shy
to walk out on anybody, even Death.
Perhaps their only motivation
was a stubborn disinclination.

Private MacNally thinking:
You squareheaded sons of bitches,
you want this God damn trench
you're going to have to take it away
from Bill McNally
of the South End of Saint John, New Brunswick.

And that's ridiculous, too, and nothing
on which to found a country.
                              Still
It makes me feel good, knowing
that in some obscure, conclusive way
they were connected with me
and me with them (65).

As I say, I do not know what Canada really gave him; but I know in my heart and soul what he gave it. He was the greatest poet of his generation, one of the few great literary figures this country has produced. But so like his literary hero Junkets, he always made an awkward bow.

I went down to visit Alden Nowlan, on that summer night long ago. Who knows, maybe to thank him. But it was too late, the curtains were drawn, and the lights were out.

He took a heart attack at his home on June 11, 1983, and, putting on old and tatter clothes that he would know from the days of his youth, walked unaided to the ambulance, just as he long ago told god he would do for Him – die with courage.

He slipped into a coma from which he never recovered, and died June 27, 1983, at the age of 50. Two years younger than I am now.

Bibliography

ARCHIVES

The three major repositories of Alden Nowlan's fonds are found in: The Alden Nowlan Papers, The Archives and Special Collections, University of Calgary Library, Calgary. The Nowlan Collection, The Special Collections at the Harriet Irving Library, University of New Brunswick, Fredericton. Clarke Irwin and Writers' Union of Canada papers, The William Ready Division of Archives and Research Collections, Mills Memorial Library, McMaster University.

WORKS BY AND ABOUT ALDEN NOWLAN
POETRY

Between Tears and Laughter: Selected Poems, Bloodaxe World Poets: 1. Tarset, UK: Bloodaxe Books, 2004.

Between Tears and Laughter. Toronto: Clarke, Irwin, 1971.

Bread, Wine and Salt. Toronto: Clarke, Irwin, 1967.

A Darkness in the Earth. Eureka, California: Hearse Press, 1959.

Early Poems. Fredericton: Fiddlehead, 1983.

An Exchange of Gifts: Poems New and Selected. Edited and with an introduction by Robert Gibbs. Toronto: Irwin, 1985.

I Might Not Tell Everybody This. Toronto: Clarke, Irwin, 1982.

The Mysterious Naked Man. Toronto: Clarke Irwin, 1969.

Playing the Jesus Game. With an introduction, "For Alden Nowlan, with Admiration," by Robert Bly: subsequently reprinted in *The Tamarack Review.* 54 (1970): 32-38; and in *Tennessee Poetry Journal.* 4.1 (1970). Trumansburg, NY: New Books, 1970.

The Rose and the Puritan. Fredericton: Fiddlehead, 1958.

Alden Nowlan: Selected Poems. Eds. Patrick Lane and Lorna Crozier. Don Mills, Ont.: House of Anansi, 1996.

Smoked Glass. Toronto: Clarke, Irwin, 1977.

I'm a Stranger Here Myself. Toronto: Clarke, Irwin, 1974.

The Things Which Are. Toronto: Contact, 1962.

Under the Ice. Toronto: Ryerson, 1961.

What Happened When He Went to the Store for Bread. Edited. With
    an introduction, "In Praise of Alden Nowlan," by Thomas
    R. Smith, with a foreword, "This Moment of Suffering and
    Confusion" by Robert Bly. Minneapolis: Nineties Press: St.
    Paul: Distributed by Ally Press Center, 1993 and [With an
    Afterword, "My Family Was Poor": *Thinking About Alden
    Nowlan and Class,"* by Thomas R. Smith] Thousands Press,
    2000.
Wind in a Rocky Country. Toronto: Emblem, 1960.

ANTHOLOGIES

Alden Nowlan and Illness. Ed. Shane Neilson. Victoria, B.C.: Frog
    Hollow Press, 2005.
The Best of Alden Nowlan. Ed. Allison Mitcham. Hantsport, N.S.:
    Lancelot, 1993.
Five New Brunswick Poets. [Elizabeth Brewster, Fred Cogswell,
    Robert Gibbs, Alden Nowlan, Kay Smith. Fredericton,
    N.B.]: Fiddlehead Poetry Books, 1962.
Shaped by This Land. With Tom Forrestall, painter. Fredericton:
    Brunswick Press: 1974.
Staying Alive: Real Poems for Unreal Times. Ed. Neil Astley. Lon-
    don: Bloodaxe Books, 2002.
Being Alive: The sequel to Staying Alive. Ed. Neil Astley. Tarset,
    UK: Bloodaxe Books, 2004.

FICTION

Miracle at Indian River. Toronto: Clarke, Irwin, 1968.
Various Persons Named Kevin O'Brien. Toronto: Clarke, Irwin,
    1973.
The Wanton Troopers. Fredericton: Goose Lane, 1988.
Will Ye Let the Mummers In? Toronto: Irwin, 1984.

ESSAYS, HISTORY, AND ADAPTATIONS

Campobello: The Outer Island. Clarke, Irwin, 1975.
Double Exposure. Fredericton, N.B.: Brunswick Press, 1978.

Nine Micmac Legends. Ills. Shirley Bear. Lancelot, 1983 [5th printing: 1987].

White Madness. Ed. Robert Gibbs. Ottawa: Oberon Press, 1996.

Road Dancers. Ed. Robert Gibbs. Ottawa: Oberon Press, 1999.

DRAMA

The Dollar Woman, with Walter Learning *New Canadian drama* 2. Ed. Patrick B. O'Neill. Borealis Press: 1981.

Frankenstein, with Walter Learning. Toronto: Clarke, Irwin, 1973.

Gardens of the Wind. [A poem for voices, CBC radio broadcast] Saskatoon: Thistledown, 1982.

The Incredible Murder of Cardinal Tosca, with Walter Learning. Toronto: Clarke, Irwin, 1978.

OTHER MEDIA
AUDIO RECORDING

Alden Nowlan's Maritimes [Maritimes: poems and short story with commentary script for CBC radio broadcast and sound recording] 1971.

The Astonishing Poems of Alden Nowlan. Readings by Robert Bly and Thomas R. Smith at Macalester College in St. Paul, Minnesota. (St. Paul: Ally Press, 1994, to mark the publication of *What Happened When He Went to the Store for read: Poems by Alden Nowlan*.

FILM

Alden Nowlan: An introduction, National Film Board of Canada, 1984.

Alden Nowlan: The Mysterious Naked Man, (Halifax: Morningtide Films, 2004).

Between Laughter and Tears, a Kent Martin film telecast by CBC's Telescope, 21 December 1972.

People's Poet: New Brunswick's Alden Nowlan, Norflicks, 2000.

ON LINE RESOURCES

Special Collections, Alden Nowlan fonds. University of Calgary
[192-], 1949-1991. 14.9 m of textual records. 34 sound
recordings. 6 photographs
http://www.ucalgary.ca/library/SpecColl/nowlana.htm

Qwerte, The University of New Brunswick Alden Nowlan Interviews, recorded commentaries offered herein are taken from
interviews conducted by Canadian filmmaker Jon Pederson
during the summer of 1982, just one year before Nowlan's
death http://www.unb.ca/qwerte/nowlan/

Athabasca University Language and Literature, Canadian Writers: biographical essays and bibliography http://www.athabas-
cau.ca/writers/nowlan/nowlan.html

Jim Stewart's Homepage, Sample Audio Recordings, including
compositions and arrangements based on the work and life
of Alden Nowlan http://personal.nbnet.nb.ca/stewart/jim-
snew.htm

Men Magazine, Real Audio Web Casts from a reading by Robert
Bly and Thomas R. Smith, editor of the first United States
anthology of Alden Nowlan's poems http://www.men-
web.org/nowlan.htm

BIBLIOGRAPHICAL RESOURCES

Moore, Jean M., Compiler; Apollonia Steele and Jean F. Tuner,
Eds. (With a biocritical essay, "Various Persons Named
Alden Nowlan," by Robert Gibbs.) *The Alden Nowlan
Papers*, University of Calgary Press (Calgary: 1992) 586 Pp.

Oliver, Michael. "Alden Nowlan (1933-83)." Lecker, Robert;
Jack David; Ellen Quigley (Eds.). *ECW's Biographical Guide
to Canadian Poets*. Toronto: ECW, 1993: 220-228.

INTERVIEWS

Choyce, Lesley. "Introduction" [Memorial] to Choyce's "Alden
Nowlan Interview" by mail two months before Nowlan's
death. *Pottersfield Portfolio* 5 (1983): 2-3.

Cockburn, Robert. An Interview in "The Alden Nowlan Special Issue." *Fiddlehead*. 81 (1969): 5-13. [Also features essays

by Ernest Buckler, Gregory Cook, Louis Dudek, Jesse Hill Ford, Anne Greer, and Edward S. (Sandy) Ives.]

Cook, Gregory. "An Interview with Alden Nowlan." *Amethyst.* 2:4 Summer (1963): 15-25.

Donnell, David. An Interview with Alden Nowlan. *Books in Canada.* June/July (1982): 26-28.

Metcalf, John. "Alden Nowlan: Interviewed by John Metcalf." *Canadian Literature.* 63 (1975): 8-17.

PUBLICATIONS ABOUT THE LIFE AND WORKS
OF ALDEN NOWLAN
BOOKS AND SPECIAL VOLUMES

Cogswell, Fred. "Alden Nowlan as Regional Atavist" in *Encounters and Explorations: Canadian Writers and European Critics.* Eds, Franz K. Stanzel and Waldemar Zacharasiewicz. Wurzburg: Konigshausen & Neumann (1986): 37-55. [Reprinted with minor revisions from *Studies in Canadian Literature.* 1:2 (Fall 1986): 206-225].

Coldford, Ian. Ed., *Pottersfield Portfolio* Vol 18. 1 (Fall 1997), "Alden Nowlan: A Reminiscence," includes tributes by Brian Bartlett, Dave Butler, Lesley Choyce, Fred Cogswell, Greg Cook, Louis Cormier, Ralph Costello, Raymond Fraser, Sharon Fraser, Leo Ferrari, Robert Gibbs, Fred Hazel, Roy MacSkimming, David Adams Richards, Thomas R. Smith, and Patrick Toner.

Cook, Gregory M. *One Heart, One Way / Alden Nowlan: a writer's life.* (With a Foreword, "The Nourishing Voice of Alden Nowlan," by Robert Bly.) Lawrencetown Beach, NS: Pottersfield Press, 2003.

Donovan, Stewart. "Surviving Shared Worlds: The Parish and the Province: Alden Nowlan and Patrick Kavanagh" in *Down East: Critical Essays on Contemporary Maritime Literature.* eds. Wolfgang Hochbuck & James Taylor. Stuttgart: Wissenchaftlicher Verlag Trier (1996): 197-208.

Howroyd, Stacey. *Alden Nowlan: A writer and poet* (reader for new literates). Literacy Council of Fredericton, 1984.

MacSkimming, Roy. "The Publishing Life," *The Perilous Trade:*

    Publishing Canada's Writers. Toronto: McClelland & Stewart 2003), 1-20.

Milton, Paul. "The Psalmist and the Sawmill: Alden Nowlan's Kevin O'Briens" in *Children's Voices in Atlantic Literature and Culture: Essays on Childhood.* Ed. Hilary Thompson. Guelph: Canadian Children's Press (1995): 60-67.

Oliver, Michael Brian. "Alden Nowlan and his works," Toronto: ECW Press, 1991.

——. *Poet's Progress: The Development of Alden Nowlan's Poetry.* Fredericton: Fiddlehead Poetry Books, 1978.

Richards, David Adams. "Lockhartville and Kevin O'Brien" [A 1987 response to the staging of a dramatization based on the fiction of Alden Nowlan] in *A Lad from Brantford and Other Essays* by David Adams Richards. Fredericton: Broken Jaw Press (1994): 36-42.

Toner, Patrick. *If I could turn and meet myself: The Life of Alden Nowlan.* Fredericton: Goose Lane Editions, 2000.

AUTOBIOGRAPHICAL SOURCES BY ALDEN NOWLAN
(IN CHRONOLOGICAL ORDER)

Scrapbook containing news clippings [*Canadian Tribune, Canadian Steelworker and Miner,* and *Windsor Tribune*]. The Alden Nowlan Papers, Calgary, 40.89.8.

"The Creation of Folks Songs," *Northeast Folklore* 1.3 Fall 1958, 48-49, Nowlan Collection, Fredericton.

"Poet in Hiding," *Nomad* 5-6 (1960) 51-52, Fiddlehead-Cogswell Collection, Fredericton.

"Alden Nowlan: Autobiographical Sketch," *Yes* 16 October 1967.

"Alden Nowlan Reports" (1968-1983) commissioned by the *Telegraph-Journal* found in Scrapbooks, Nowlan Collection, Fredericton, and in The Alden Nowlan Papers, Calgary, 40.1041-40.107.3.

"Alden Nowlan's Canada," *Maclean's* June 1971, 15-17, 40.

"Hatfield Country," *Maclean's,* November 1971, 41-42, 76-78.

"Something to Write About," *Canadian Literature* Nos. 68-69 Spring-Summer 1976

"Growing Up in Katpesa Creek," in *Double Exposure,* p. 17, Brunswick Press, Fredericton, NB, 1978.

"A Bubble Dancer and The Wickedest Man in Carleton County,"
   The Fiddlehead 125 Spring 1980, 75-77.

"What About the Irvings?," *Canadian Newspapers: The Inside
   Story*, edited by Walter Stewart. Hurtig, Edmonton: 1980.

"By Celestial Omnibus to the Twilight Zone," *Fiddlehead* 136
   June 1983.

ARTICLES BY OTHERS

Anonymous, Editor's memorial introduction to Alden Nowlan's
   short story, "About Memorials," published posthumously in
   The Fiddlehead. 137 (1983): 20.

Baxter, Marilyn. "Wholly Drunk or Wholly Sober?" *Canadian
   Literature*. 68-69 (1976): 106-11.

Bieman, Elizabeth. "Wrestling with Nowlan's Angel." *Canadian
   Poetry*. 2(1978):43-50. www.arts.uwo.ca/canpoetry/cpjrn/
   vol02/bieman.htm

Bruce, Harry. "Alden Nowlan January 25, 1933 – June 27,
   1983," *Atlantic Insight,* August 1983, 17.

Bryson, Michael. "TDR Interview: Gregory M. Cook," *The
   Danforth Review*. http://www.danforthreview.com/fea-
   tures/interviews/gregory'm'cook.htm

Cameron, Silver Donald. "The Poet from Desolation Creek,"
   Saturday Night, May 1973, 28-31.

Cook, Geoffrey. Rev. of *Alden Nowlan: Selected Poems* by Alden
   Nowlan, *Pottersfield Portfolio*. Winter 1997 (Vol 17, No 2),
   84-87.

Cook, Greg. "Alden Nowlan: Something rare and beautiful," *New
   Brunswick Reader*. 29 April (1995): 9-12. http://www.athabas-
   cau.ca/writers/nowlan/rare.html

——."One Heart, One Way: a life of Alden Nowlan," *Nashwaak
   Review*. Fall (1996): 173-179.

——. "The wine of astonishment: lines in the life of New
   Brunswick's national poet." *New Brunswick Reader*. 27 June
   (1998): 5-8. http://personal.nbnet.nb.ca/cookgreg/pages/
   memories.htm

——. "Imposing Order / Poet's Class Work: a bio-critical
   glimpse of Alden Nowlan 1933-1983," [2001]. / /http://
   www.athabascau.ca/writers/nowlan/order.html

Djwa, Sandra. "Alden Nowlan: 1933-83." *Canadian Literature.* 101 (1984): 180-183.

Fetherling, Douglas. "Guiding Lights," *Books in Canada* Oct 1994, 61.

Fraser, Keath. "Notes on Alden Nowlan." *Canadian Literature.* 45 (1970): 41-51.

Jones, Ted. "Alden Nowlan: Required Reading," *New Brunswick*, Vol. 8, No. 3-4 [Fredericton: New Brunswick Information Service], 1978.

Mandel, Ann. "Useful Fictions: Legends of the Self in Roth, Blaise, Kroetsch, and Nowlan." *Ontario Review: A North American Journal of the Arts.* 3 (1975): 26-32.

Manzer, Susan. "Christmas is the Time," *Daily Gleaner* 22 Dec 1972.

Melnyk, Helen. "Our Alden Talks, Coughs, Hacks – And Wins The West," *The Telegraph Journal,* 1 April 1978.

Milton, Paul. "*Various Persons Named Kevin O'Brien*: Nowlan's Novel Response to the Critics." *Studies in Canadian Literature.* 23 (1998): 36-48.

Richards, David Adams. "I Went to Meet Alden Nowlan," *The Globe & Mail* 21 June, 2003 R1, 5.

Scott, Virginia. "'Down Shore': Alden Nowlan's Poetry in the late Sixties." *American Review of Canadian Studies.* 22.1 (Spring 1992): 23-38.

Tyrwhitt, Janice. "The Man from Desolation Creek, *Readers' Digest*, March 1984, 67-71.

Ustick, Michael. "Repression: The Poetry of Alden Nowlan." Canadian Literature. 60 (1974): 43-50.

Van Wart, Alice. "Spreading Nowlan's words," *The Globe & Mail* 26 June 1993, C4.

THESIS /

DISSERTATIONS ON THE WORK OF ALDEN NOWLAN

Balsom, Edwin James. "Dialogic regional voices: A study of selected contemporary Atlantic-Canadian fiction (Alden Nowlan, Susan Kerslake, John Steffler, David Adams Richards). "Dissertation (PhD), Memorial University of Newfoundland, 1999.

Callbeck, Janette Ellen, "Journey toward scepticism: The novels of Alden Nowlan." Thesis (MA), Acadia University, 1998.

Cormier, Audrey M. "Regionalism in the fiction of Alistair MacLeod, Alden Nowlan, and David Adams Richards." Thesis (M.A.), University of New Brunswick, Dept. of English, 2000.

Greer, Anne Johnston. "Alienation and affirmation in the work of Alden Nowlan." Thesis (M.A.), Acadia University, 1973.

Jacquot, Martine. "Dream as an escape in Alden Nowlan's fiction." Thesis (MA) Acadia University, 1986.

Lawson, Craig Paul. "Empty strength and throttled rage: Social class immobility in the poetry and prose of Alden Nowlan." Thesis (M.A.) University of Calgary, 2000.

Manitt, Orin. "The changing perception of time as an index of heroic venture in the poetry of Alden Nowlan." Thesis (M.A.), Concordia University, 1984.

Steeves, Winston Andrew. "Alden Nowlan's letters to Raymond Fraser: 1961-1977." Thesis (M.A.), Acadia University, 1996.

Toner, Patrick. "The passionate profane: puritanism and paganism in the poetry of Alden Nowlan." Thesis (M.A.), Carleton University, 1993.

Zanes, John Page, "Where the Fiddleheads Grow And the Wind Blows Blue: A Consideration of a Canadian Literary Tradition." Dissertation (PhD), The University of Texas at Austin, 1979.

List of Contributors

Geoffrey Cook lives in Montreal and teaches English at John Abbot College. His reviews have appeared in various Canadian journals, particularly TheDanforthReview.com, where he was a poetry editor. His poems have also been widely published, including in the anthologies of Atlantic Canadian poetry, *Landmarks* (2001) and *Coastlines* (2002). His first book is *Postscript* (Véhicule Press/Signal Editions, 2004).

Gregory M. Cook lives in Saint John. His intimate biography, *One Heart, One Way / Alden Nowlan: a writer's life* (Pottersfield Press), was short-listed for two 2004 Atlantic Writing Awards – the Booksellers' Choice and the Dartmouth Book Award. His book of new and selected poems is *Songs of the Wounded* (Black Moss Press, 2004).

John Metcalf lives and writes in Ottawa. The Senior Editor at the Porcupine's Quill Press and a prolific anthologist, he is also the author of more than a dozen works of fiction and non-fiction. His most recent books are *An Aesthetic Underground: a literary memoir* (Thomas Allen) and the fiction *Forde Aboard* (Porcupine's Quill).

Paul Milton specializes in post-war Canadian and American fiction at Okanagan University College, Kelowna. His publications include articles on Leonard Cohen, George Eliot, and Alden Nowlan – including "The Psalmist and the

Sawmill: (see the bibliography here) and the forthcoming: "'Nowhere So Dark as in the Country Where I was Born': Alden Nowlan and the Home Place."

David Adams Richards lives in Toronto. A Giller Prize Winner for *Mercy Among the Children* and twice a Governor General's Award Winner – for one of his Miramichi trilogy, *Nights Below Station Street* – and for non-fiction (*Lines on the Water*), David was a close friend of Alden Nowlan from the beginning of his career. His latest novel is *River of the Brokenhearted* (Double Day Canada).

Thomas R. Smith is a poet, editor, and reviewer living in River Falls, Wisconsin. Besides selecting Alden Nowlan's poems for US readers in *What Happened When He Went to the Store for Bread* (Thousands Press), he has seen three of his own books of poems into print, most *recently The Dark Indigo Current* (Holy Cow! Press).

Printed in October 2006
at Gauvin Press, Gatineau, Québec